THE PRO-T OFFENSE: WINNING FOOTBALL WITH A MODERN PASSING ATTACK

ABOUT THE AUTHOR

Mike McDaniels is currently the head football coach at Stanley-Boyd (WI) High School. During his 5-year term, his "Pro-T" has shattered 57 school records, and in 1981 produced the most explosive offense in the school's history. During this time he was selected as Class B District I "Coach of the Year."

As head football coach at Grantsburg (WI) High School, he installed the Pro-T attack and took Grantsburg (9–0) to its first state playoff game and was chosen Class C District I, "Coach of the Year."

McDaniels has also served as an assistant at the University of Wisconsin, River Falls, and Hudson (WI) High School.

Coach McDaniels has written articles for such magazines as *The Athletic Journal, Wisconsin Interscholastic Athletic Association Bulletin,* and *The Wisconsin High School Football Coaches Association Newsletter.*

THE PRO-T OFFENSE: WINNING FOOTBALL WITH A MODERN PASSING ATTACK

Mike McDaniels

Parker Publishing Company, Inc.
West Nyack, New York

© 1984 by

PARKER PUBLISHING COMPANY, INC.

West Nyack, N.Y.

Library of Congress Cataloging in Publication Data

McDaniels, Mike.
  The pro-T offense.

  Includes index.
  1. Football—Offense.   2. Football—Coaching.
I. Title.
GV951.8.M33   1984   796.332'2   84-9414

ISBN 0-13-731225-3

Printed in the United States of America

To my wife, Paula, and our daughters, Annie and Mary.
To my parents, Mr. and Mrs. LaVerne H. McDaniels.
To my father-in-law and mother-in-law, Dr. and Mrs. Nick S.
Dzubay.

ACKNOWLEDGMENTS

There is no doubt in my mind that I would not have chosen the teaching and coaching profession if it were not for those coaches in the Janesville, Wisconsin, Public School System. Their professionalism, enthusiasm, and dedication have given many student athletes many memorable and exciting years.

Very few coaches would ever be successful if it weren't for the assistant coaches who have given generously of their time for the betterment of others. I have been very fortunate in working with such fine gentlemen as Jim Brinker, Steve Johnson, Clayton Jorgenson, Lee LaFlamme, Bob Olson, and Mark Smith. Their experience and creativity have made this offense a reality.

I am very grateful to the *Athletic Journal* Magazine Company for their publications of many of my articles. Their publications have inspired me to write this book—*The Pro-T Offense: Winning Football with a Modern Passing Attack.*

HOW THIS BOOK WILL HELP
YOUR OFFENSIVE ATTACK

The pro-T attack is one of the most explosive offenses ever put together. The combination of two wide receivers and a tight end gives this offense both short and long range passing capability. Within the pro-T arsenal is the ability to score points when needed. Coaches can also use this attack for the purpose of ball control.

The pro-T appears in the form of a strategic manual rather than a play book. It goes beyond showing only the basic plays involved in one's offense. You obtain a strategic insight for which formations best suit your purpose, where the total attack should be directed, and what you should be looking for and thinking about as the game progresses. In short, you are given a sideline view as a member of the coaching staff, gaining the knowledge of this attack as if you were there calling the plays.

This offense uses the concept of multiple formations. These sets are used to alter and offset any discrepancies between the offense and your opponent. Through the use of a multiformation pro-type offense, you have the capability to control the defense by forcing the opponent to make key adjustments that best suit your game plan. With the multiple formation system, other devices are used to manipulate both the linebackers and defensive backs. Motion can be added to this system in order to flood one specific area of the field, as well as being used as a decoy to force a commitment by the defense.

This offense uses several series. These include such basic plays as the dive, sweep, off tackle, quick pitch, and various forms of trap plays. Out of each series are a multitude of options that can be used to make a simple play more versatile and effective. With the introduction of the drop-back, roll-out, and play-action passing, these base plays can be explosive enough to offset any defense. The basic running attack is not hampered by an overbearing passing game, nor do you have to run the ball simply to keep the defense honest.

The pro-T is designed with many built-in options. These systems give the athlete the option to make decisions in critical situations. Each phase of the offense, from line blocking to running a pass pattern, uses several basic keys. These keys are read by each member of the offense and are used to offset unforeseen occurrences, such as blitzing linebackers, slanting linemen, defensive end play, and prerotations in secondary coverages.

Without a doubt, the greatest advantage of the pro-T offense is its tremendous capability of putting points on the scoreboard. Its balanced attack and multiple formation system prevent defenses from keying on any one player or area of the team. No longer will weather or the loss of one key player limit the offense in its ultimate goal.

One of the greatest characteristics of the pro-T is that it can be introduced into any level of your program. With a systematic progression, this offense can be built on from the basic to the most complex. By adding to your player's knowledge each year, the varsity athlete will have the complete understanding of the strategy used in this attack.

The versatility of this offense enables you to win with average players. Being realistic, you know that many games are won by the team with the greatest amount of talent. Very few offenses are flexible enough to be used successfully by teams with limited size and ability. The successful execution of this offense does not depend on the exceptionally talented athletes. Quick teams, lacking in size can benefit as well as the large, overwhelming and powerful team.

In this book, you will obtain the knowledge and strategy needed to spice up your offense. Field strategies are covered, allowing you to experience how effective the pro-T can be, before it becomes a reality. You will find that this book includes more than just the pro-T formation offense. Many formations are included with descriptions of how their use can be effective.

Through many years of experience, built-in systems have been installed to alter problems which you may face from year to year.

Above all, you will have the complete understanding of how this offense works and of how productive it can be. Lack of talent, weather conditions and an unfavorable outlook towards the coming season, can be overcome with the use of this exciting, self-motivating, and explosive offense.

Mike McDaniels

CONTENTS

1

ADVANTAGES
OF THE PRO-T
ATTACK

With 17 years of football experience, I have had the opportunity to come in contact with a wide variety of offenses. Each of these offenses had sound and basic principles in the philosophy of moving the football. Few, however, have had as much overall success as the pro-T attack.

The concept of the pro-T offense is not a new one. However, with the takeover success that the passing game has had, more and more coaches are realizing that keeping up with the times may include using the pro-T.

With the explosiveness of the passing game, through the use of the two wide receivers and tight end, defenses are now forced to play at least a three-deep secondary. By incorporating one or both of the halfbacks into a specific pattern, the offense has changed the attitude of the linebackers from one of run support to one of becoming more pass conscious and drop zone protective.

The pro-T running game is based on the concept of a series of plays, rather than scattering plays from one side of the formation to the other. Each series contains several optional plays designed to attack specific weak areas of the defense. These variations within the base series look very similar in their execution but have ultimately different effects. Through the use of the drop-back, roll-out, and play-action passing incorporated into each series, one basic series can provide you with more offensive punch than the defense can adjust to.

Multiple formations have given the basic pro-T alignment more than the three-receiver concept. If and when your basic one-formation attack fails to direct defensive change, a new and even more explosive formation can be used to single out specific defensive weaknesses. These various types of formations are used to alter and offset any physical disadvantages that your offense will face. These formations may be used as an excellent two-minute offense or changed to force the defense into another alignment.

With the flexibility that has been built into this system, you no longer have to wait for the "blue chip" team to come along. With eight years of experience using this offense, we have arrived at a system that can meet the needs of every athlete. Each phase of this attack has built-in options. These options allow athletes to make decisions that will better their overall performance in a given situation. With the talented athlete, this offense can put you far above the rest of your competitors. Even with below-average talent, the pro-T can make your team every bit as competitive as your rivals.

OFFENSIVE THEORY

In order to be successful at any level of football, the offense must maintain a certain level of consistency. In order to do this, the offense must control the defense with whatever means are within their capability.

The pro-T relies on the concept of defensive manipulation. Many offensives use the same concept, but where the pro-T differs is in its overall approach of taking what it wants, rather than being passive and taking what the defense gives up. This theory is based on the execution of play progression against specific types of defenses. Through this progression, the pro-T concentrates its efforts on attacking one specific area of the field, or specific group of defenders.

In attacking these defensive weaknesses, the offense can use this working progression to offset and alter possible defensive changes that occur. By integrating each individual play into this progression, you will know exactly what the defense will do to stop this progression before their readjustments are made. This working knowledge allows you to add to the already working effects of your attack.

The pro-T uses five basic principles in attacking any defense. Through these five principles you have the understanding of how this offense uses its talents in attacking defensive weaknesses to suit its needs.

Attacking the Defense

One of the major attributes that the pro-T possesses is the ability to spread the defense. Each formation used in this offense forces the defense to give up specific areas of the field. These vulnerable areas are targeted and referred to as the attack zones. With the spreading of the defense, the pro-T concentrates on those areas that are unoccupied by the defense. All offensive efforts are made to force the defense into making a total commitment to supporting these weak areas.

In attacking any defense, the first plays used in the progression must be geared to work on the open zones. Further plays will be designed specifically to attack defensive adjustments that take place within this area.

Looking at a three-deep zone, one can see the open areas between the two defensive corners and middle safety (see Figure 1.1). These areas are attacked with various types of pass patterns. The progression of plays used depends on whether or not the defense commits itself to stopping the first series of passing plays into this vulnerable area. The pass patterns themselves aren't as important as the size of the area being attacked. The quick slant, button hook, curl, and short square-in can be used as a starting point, but our main concern when attacking any area is, how will the defense adjust?

From looking at Figure 1.1, you realize that the outside linebackers have to be used in the defense of the attack area if a pass is thrown. This cuts down their effectiveness in supporting the run, but it adds to the pass coverage in the open zone. With the outside linebacker reading pass first, his stunting

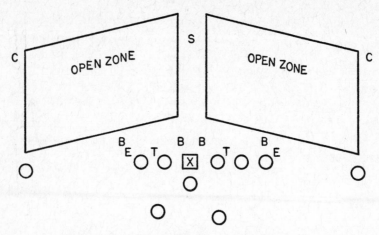

Figure 1.1 Open Area Vs. 3-Deep Zone.

ability is also limited. You, as the offensive coach, now realize that one or both of the halfbacks is not needed as additional pass blockers. This coverage by the linebackers allows you to put at least one of the running backs into a play that specifically attacks the vulnerable area.

To show how the progression works, the offense attacks the open zone with a short post pattern to the flanker. The flanker penetrates the open zone between the corner and safety. By completing patterns of this type several times in a row, the outside linebacker has to position himself in an area between the safety and defensive corner. With the possibility of an outside stunt gone, the right halfback can now be freed up to execute a loop pattern in the flats area (see Figure 1.2).

As the progression continues, different adjustments are used in order to pick up the looping back who has come out of the backfield. The defense now has the option of moving the playside linebacker out wider in order to pick up the loop receiver or bring up the corner in a man-to-man technique on the halfback. In order to outguess the defense, two patterns are used in the event that one of the two adjustments is being employed. The tight end executes a delay-5 pattern. This pattern delays the tight end into the outside curl zone between the playside outside linebacker and the middle linebacker. In the event that the outside linebacker is picking up the loop re-

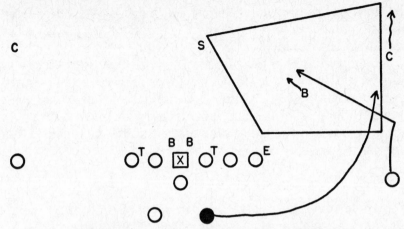

Figure 1.2   Attacking the Open Area with the Halfback.

ceiver, the tight end will be open. The flanker, who has been running an inside type of pattern, now executes an X-go. This pattern is somewhat like the Z-out except it starts from a basic post pattern instead of a slanting pattern (see Figure 1.3).

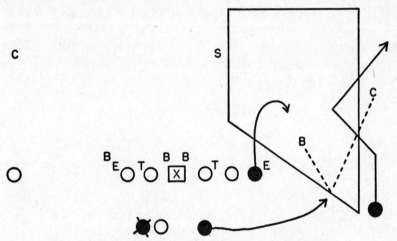

Figure 1.3   Taking Advantage of the Linebacker Adjustment.

When attacking a specific area, you may come across defenses that do not adjust to your progression of plays. In that case, stop the progression momentarily and continue to flood this open zone with the same patterns over and over again until the defense has to make a change. At the time of the defensive change, you begin the progression and work on the adjustments that have been made.

The principle of the progression attack allows you to dictate the strategy and positioning of the defense. In attempting to stop this overload in one zone, the defense opens up an even larger zone on the opposite size of the formation. Once this opening has been enlarged, the offense shifts its attack to this unguarded area.

Attacking Zone Coverages

Zone coverages work on the concept of dropping defenders into a specific area as fast as possible and then waiting for the pass to be thrown. This allows the members of the zone to get a better picture of the play as it develops.

In attacking zone coverages, two areas must be considered. First, since the defenders are already in position to cover the pass, they have already made a commitment by dropping into their respective zones. By committing themselves, the defense has allowed the offense to put several receivers into those zones and has enabled the receivers to outnumber the defenders. This is done through the use of flood patterns. One receiver clears out the deep zone so that another receiver can work himself free in the unoccupied area of the under zone (see Figure 1.4).

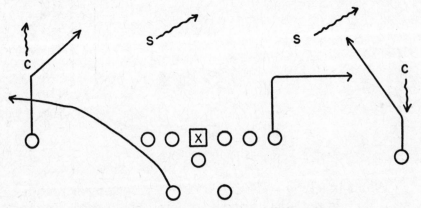

Figure 1.4   Attacking the Under Zones with Flood Patterns.

Normally, the four-deep zone coverage has a specific rotation. This rotation may be predetermined or set up to rotate on the movement of the play action itself. In determining where the rotation is taking place, the quarterback merely reads the playside defensive corner. The corner's initial movement tells the quarterback where run support is coming from, and who is responsible for picking up the short under zone in the flats area. The actual reading, which takes place when playing against zone coverages, is discussed more in-depth in Chapter 4.

The second area of concern when attacking a zone defense deals with the linebackers. As you know, linebacker drops are designed to fill empty holes left in the under zones, as well as used as a buffer between the line of scrimmage and the deep defenders. The drops that are taken by the linebackers give the offense two options. The offense may either execute patterns that divide the deep zones of the secondary and the short zones of the linebackers, or it can use the flooding type of patterns specifically designed to offset the linebacker coverage.

The first option, dividing deep zones, requires that a pass be thrown under the deep coverage of the secondary and over

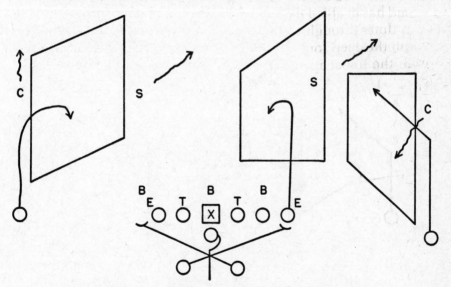

Figure 1.5 Play Action Will Hold Linebackers from Making Their Drops.

the coverage of the linebackers. This type of pass is more difficult since the pass has to be precise in its execution. In order to make this type of pass more effective, play-action passing should be used to hold the linebacker in place as long as possible. The play action prevents the linebackers from getting to their drops quickly, allowing them to set up (see Figure 1.5).

The second alternative when throwing against the combination of the deep and short coverages, is to execute patterns that are isolated on one specific linebacker in that particular zone. When isolating on one linebacker, a combination of several patterns must be run directly into his zone. One receiver must chase the deep corner out of position so that no help can come from the outside. Inside support comes from the playside safety. Knowing this, a curl pattern is executed by the slot receiver to hold the outside linebacker in place. With the off-tackle action to the slot side, the left halfback continues into the flats. The outside linebacker is outnumbered in his zone. If he picks up the curl receiver, the halfback will be open, and if he picks up the halfback, the curl zone will be unprotected (see Figure 1.6).

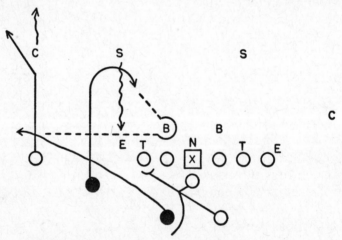

Figure 1.6   Isolating on the Playside Linebacker.

Although zone coverages are more difficult to attack than the man-to-man type, flooding a group of receivers into a specific zone can be used effectively to outnumber the defenders. Flooding can take place with the use of picks, loops, flares, and delay patterns. A more direct explanation is given for the use of these patterns in Chapter 4.

Attacking Man-to-Man Coverages

The man-to-man secondary coverages pit the ability of one man against another. Coaches who use this type of defensive play feel confident that their athletes do a better job in stopping the pass than the offensive receivers do in catching it. In order to give the receiver the edge, man-to-man coverages are attacked with the pick, isolation, and delay series. Each of these three types of passes gives the defender an opportunity to take himself out of every play.

The pick series works on the same concept as the pick in basketball. One defender is screened out to enable another member of the offense to work himself open.

Isolation patterns affect the man-to-man defense because these patterns are executed so quickly and accurately that the individual defender is unable to react fast enough to cover the play. Once the defender has committed himself in stopping the isolation pattern, a go adjustment can be added to the base series. This adjustment gives the receiver an additional pattern change that puts the defender in an even more difficult position.

The delay series works on the same basic principle as the isolation series, except the delay patterns are executed after the defensive back has moved out of position. By delaying any one receiver into a specific pattern, he has the time and opportunity to read the initial movement of his foe. This gives the receiver a chance to select the pattern that will work best in a given situation.

Motion has proven to be extremely successful when used against man-to-man coverage. It forces each defender to overlap his individual coverage of each receiver. This overlap allows the receiver to work himself open more rapidly and put the defenders in a position where they are no longer capable of covering their receivers effectively.

Attacking the Linebackers

Like any offense, the pro-T is also faced with the threat of the all-out linebacker blitz. Blitzing can be effectively controlled with the quick series motion and the use of the multiple formation system.

The quick patterns, evolved from the quick series, are designed to hit the areas of the field that have been left vacant by the blitzing linebackers. Plays within the quick series can be prearranged in the huddle if a blitz is suspected or on the line of scrimmage through the audible check-off system.

The multiple formation offense forces the linebackers out of their normal position and changes their role from run support to pass coverage. This limits the amount of stunting that can take place by any one defense. Very few defenses have the confidence to defend these formations with a seven- or eight-man front. Instead you will be looking at a much more conservative type of defensive alignment, one that is designed to cover the spread of the formation, rather than defend the offense.

With the additional use of motion, linebacker responsibilities are changed drastically. Motion can strengthen or weaken any one side of the offensive formation. This puts additional pressure on the outside linebackers and forces them to take a different view of motion and how it will affect their responsibilities. Motion in the pro-T can tighten up or open up a specific passing area of the field. By widening the area that the linebackers are responsible for, their effectiveness in stopping the run and pass becomes more difficult. These pattern series are designed to put the linebackers in a truly defensive position and limit them to the amount of blitzing that they are capable of performing.

Attacking in the Trenches

Of these five areas, the defensive line is the only area that takes full advantage of the five principles used in attacking the defense. In attacking the defensive line, combination blocking, along with the false split system, is used to offset any size and skill imbalance that may exist between our offensive line and our opponents' defensive front.

The combination blocking system enables each member of the offensive line to take full advantage of his individual skills. If a defender cannot be moved out of a specific hole purely by the use of force, other mental compensations can be made in order to perform this task. An example of mental compensation is multiple formations. Multiple formations have a great deal to do with the overall positioning of the defensive line. By spreading out the secondary and linebacker personnel, the defensive line is faced with the possible situation of being outnumbered in the trenches. In many cases, the total spreading of any defensive line gives the offensive line the opportunity of double-teaming any specific hole or setting up trapping schemes when faced with an overly aggressive front. You will find that the spreading of any formation results in the two-philosophy defense.

Since the offense is in an overwhelming position to dominate the line of scrimmage, the defenders may be reading the initial play as it develops before making any commitment. This, in effect, gives the offensive line a jump on the snap count and quick-hitting plays can be effectively executed with simple blocking schemes. The other type of philosophy deals with the all-out pass rush or aggressive defensive front. The defense may be attacking with every ounce of energy it has. By changing the types of pass protection from roll out, to drop back, to play action, the overly aggressive defense is forced to slow their charge momentarily to prevent themselves from being taken out of the play.

OPTIMISTIC OUTLOOK WITH THE PRO-T ATTACK

Very few coaches can argue that the pro-T attack has become the most sought after offense of our era. Practically every major football power in the United States has tried to develop some kind of offense that simulates the overall explosiveness of the pro-T. We are not talking about the pro-T formation with the three basic receivers who are used as decoys to set up a stubborn ground-oriented offense; we are talking about an all out blitzkrieg.

The pro-T relies on total control of the defense through the use of a multiple formation offense that can totally dictate the placement of each individual defender. These formations can supply ample passing power as well as sustain a powerful and effective running attack.

Despite having as much offense as any one coach can handle, the pro-T is based on only a limited number of basic plays that have the capability of becoming more effective through the use of play-action, drop-back, and roll-out passing.

Unlike some offenses, this attack is geared to meet the needs of the athletes. Every athlete has the chance to pit his skills against an opponent with the use of built-in options. These options allow the player to make judgments concerning his particular skill level and provide each athlete with alternate choices. No longer is an athlete expected to do the impossible. The entire pro-T system is put together with the sole purpose of taking advantage of whatever talent exists.

2

SELECTING PERSONNEL FOR THE PRO-T ATTACK

In the selection of personnel used in this offense, each position describes what the coaching staff should be looking for in an athlete. As most coaches experience, more seasons are spent in instructing average players, rather than a squad of blue chippers. Talent may vary drastically from one player to the next, but to win you must find the best 11 players and mold them into a workable machine. In selecting personnel you will find that no matter how grim the season may look, the players on your team may fit into the mold needed to put this attack into a workable reality.

THE CENTER (C)

The offensive center is sometimes an overlooked position. The responsibility of putting the ball into play can mean the difference between winning and losing.

The selection of the center should be made at the earliest level of the athletes' involvement in the program. This may be the fifth, sixth, or as late as the ninth grade, depending on your feeder program. Our belief is that once a player is a center, he's always a center.

When selecting the athlete as a center, intelligence and leadership are the major qualities you should look for. Because of the importance of the ball exchange between the center and the quarterback, the center should range in height between 5 feet 10 inches and 6 feet. Most centers should weigh at least 160 pounds, but extremely tough kids that weigh 150 pounds can qualify for this position. The common trait which all linemen should share is quickness. As you will see in the blocking scheme, a quick sting is more effective than a slow push. Because of the screen-blocking techniques used in the offensive line-blocking system, strength and overall speed are not as important as quickness in the center position.

THE GUARDS (G)

Of all the interior line positions, the two most talented individuals must be the guards. They must be strong enough to block defensive tackles when playing against an even front and quick enough to cut off the pursuing linebackers when up against an odd alignment. With the amount of pulling and trapping that is done by these two talented athletes, quickness and overall speed are necessary. In the selection of the guard positions, size has never been a prerequisite. If the small guard has all the qualities mentioned above, he will do an effective job of blocking. The pro-T attack does not have a weak or strong guard description. Both guards should possess equal ability. When coaching the guards, make sure that they spend an equal amount of time in practice working both sides of the offensive line.

THE TACKLES (T)

It is sometimes said that the strength of every good football team lies in its tackles. This statement is very true in the pro-T attack. The tackles in this offense have to be very physical, both in strength and aggressiveness. The tackles are generally the heaviest players on the interior line. Because they may be playing against larger defensive tackles, they must have better-than-average quickness. Overall speed is not as important as the ability to pull on the quick pitch. They should be able to think quickly and react to picking up defenders downfield. As in the guard positions, both tackles should be able to play on either side.

THE TIGHT END (Y)

Normally the tight end is your overall biggest receiver and should be the best blocker. Because of the amount of blocking that the tight end must do, he must be durable enough to seal block on defensive tackles and quick enough to pick up the pursuing linebackers.

The tight end is also involved in about 90 percent of all pass plays and should possess better-than-average speed, quickness, and agility. His involvement in the passing game dictates that he have good hands and can take the physical punishment dealt out by the defensive secondary. In many cases, this position may be filled by your best all-around athlete, possibly one of your team captains.

THE SPLIT END (X)

In the pro-T offense, the split end is generally on the opposite side of the tight end and flanker. Because of this, he roams in a much larger area of the field. Of all the offensive positions, the split end should exhibit the best overall speed and quickness.

Along with speed and quickness, this player must have sure hands. The split end has to be durable and able to take blind side hits, which often plague the player of this position. Because of the amount of responsibility the receiver has, this athlete must also be intelligent and flexible enough to make snap decisions concerning his pattern as the play develops.

Many split ends have all the tools but lack one important ingredient: basic football knowledge. An athlete may have average physical qualities, but if he possesses good football sense he can play this position as well as anyone.

THE FLANKER (Z) (4)

Despite the many roles a flanker is asked to perform, his may be one of the easiest positions to fill. In selecting this position you may find an athlete who is a borderline starter at either the split end or halfback positions. If he possesses qualities at both positions, he would certainly qualify as a flanker.

In the pro-T attack the flanker is primarily a receiver and should have good hands. There will be cases when the flanker will be called on to carry the ball, so he should be physically tough enough to withstand the same contact that a running back would take. The flanker, like the split end, should have good speed.

Size is not a pressing concern in the flanker position, though you may be looking for an athlete who stands 6 feet 3 inches tall and weighs 210 pounds. The same type of rugged athlete with the will to play, the ability to catch and run with the ball, could be just the player for flanker.

THE BACKS

Left Halfback (L) (2) and
Right Halfback (R) (3)

For the most explosive pro-T attack, both backs should possess similar qualities. Two backs who balance each other are more effective than the 1 to 3 yards and a cloud of dust type, or the type who is strictly a sweep or outside man.

The backs should obviously have better-than-average speed. You should look for athletes with a 4.8 or 5.0 time in the 40-yard dash. Faster backs make the offense more patient and allow a wider range of play selection. The pro-T offense requires the backs to do quite a bit of blocking for each other. Therefore, a rugged, tough, and aggressive type of athlete should be selected.

Halfbacks are often used as receivers in the passing attack. These individuals should be able to catch the football and know the patterns and formations that are involved.

THE QUARTERBACK (QB)(1)

Like the center's position, the quarterback is selected from the earliest level of competition. By the time he reaches the varsity level of play, he should know and understand all facets of the attack, including what plays are most successful against certain defenses and how to use the potential of the offense to its fullest.

The quarterback is the general on the field. He should be the take charge type of player. Because of the number of passes thrown in a specific game, a strong arm is very important. The quarterback should be at least 5 feet 10 inches tall in order to be in a natural, relaxed position when taking the snap. The quarterback should have at least average speed and above-average quickness, as he is involved in a number of running plays. This may sound like a hard position to fill, but by starting boys out at an early age, you'll make your job easier as a coach and make the offense a more potent weapon.

3

SYSTEM BASICS USED IN THE PRO-T OFFENSE

This chapter deals with the introduction of the offensive formations and their numbering system. These formations are given with their strategic use in mind. The placement and function of the backfield sets are also explained. Play calling is given in its entirety, and motion is discussed as a strategic advantage.

FORMATIONS USED IN THE PRO-T ATTACK

The pro-T consists of more than the use of the pro-T formation. This offense uses a wide variety of alignments to counterbalance defensive formations. Each of these formations has a specific philosophy behind it. Not all the formations discussed are used in every game, but each is practiced in case its use is necessary. By not using all these formations in every game, your opponents will not be able to scout your offense completely. It should be noted that many of these formations require major defensive changes for effective coverage. These changes force your opponents into playing a specific defense that they are unaccustomed to.

The Pro Set

The pro-T formation, with its two wide receivers and tight end, is the primary set used in this attack. With the two outside receivers and inside positioning by the tight end, the defense is forced into playing at least a three-man secondary. By using one, or both of the running backs, you have the potential of sending five eligible receivers into a pass pattern.

The pro set can be called to either direction. The formations are called pro right and pro left. The pro right call puts the flanker and tight end on the right and the split end on the left, and the pro left flips the formation over (see Figures 3.1 and 3.2).

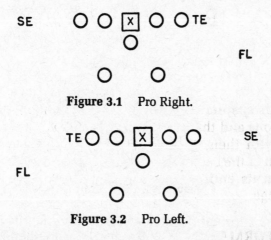

Figure 3.1   Pro Right.

Figure 3.2   Pro Left.

The pro formation is used against every type of defense. It is a well-rounded set in its effectiveness when running or passing. As an offense, we do not move out of this formation unless we were unable to move the ball successfully on the ground or through the air. If we are successful with either one or the other, we remain in this set and start using motion, or shift backfield sets to create an overload to one side.

The Slot Formation

The slot formation is an adjustment made from the base formation. The slot allows the offense to flood one side of the formation with two receivers. When pick and isolation patterns are used, this formation is very effective against teams that play man-to-man in the secondary.

The slot can be started as a normal formation, or the flanker can go in motion out of the pro set towards the split end and become the slot man before the snap. Like the pro-T, the slot is called to the side where it will be used. The slot-right call puts the split end and flanker on the right side. The split end is positioned between 10 and 12 yards from the offensive tackle. The flanker lines up 1 yard off the ball and splits the difference between the split end and the tackle. The tight end always lines up on the opposite side (see Figures 3.3 and 3.4).

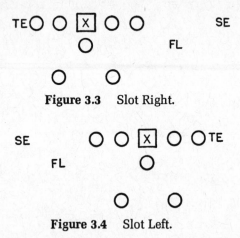

Figure 3.3   Slot Right.

Figure 3.4   Slot Left.

The slot formation also adds to the effectiveness of the running game. A receiver in the slot has a good blocking angle for any outside plays. This formation also has the potential of hitting the defense with an inside counter and reverse from the slot position.

The Double Slot and Double Twins

The double slot and double twins formations are basically the same. Their effectiveness may vary according to the way in which the defense adjusts to the two formations.

The double slot-right formation puts the split end and flanker on the right side. As in the normal slot, these splits will be 10 to 12 yards for the split end and 5 to 6 yards for the flanker. The left side of the double slot right will position the tight end split at 10 to 12 yards and the left halfback at 5 to 6. The mirror formation is the double slot left. The split end and flanker are positioned to the left side, using the same splits as those on the right. The tight end and right halfback make up the slot on the other side.

When using this formation, you may bring in another wide receiver to take the place of your tight end. This decision depends on the speed and ability of your tight end (see Figures 3.5 and 3.6).

Figure 3.5   Double Slot Right.

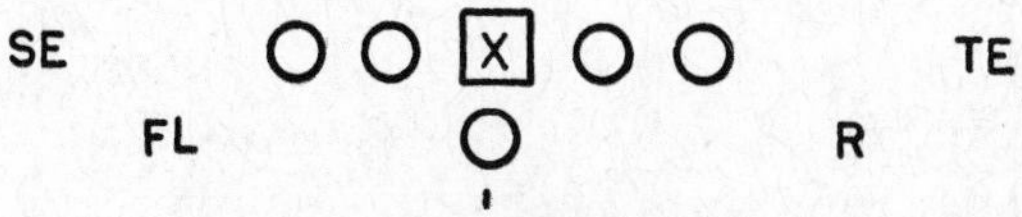

Figure 3.6   Double Slot Left.

The double slot is an offense within itself. This formation has been commonly referred to as the run and gun offense. The double slot draws the coverage of the outside linebackers. When linebackers are positioned head up on the slot receivers, the loop and pick series can be used to give the linebackers more than they can handle.

The double twins position and the direction or side where it is to be used is given exactly the same as the double slot. The only difference is that in the double twins both receivers are right next to each other with a 1-yard split separating them (see Figures 3.7 and 3.8).

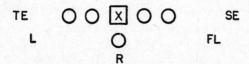

Figure 3.7   Double Twins Right.

These two formations are basically used against teams that play a 4–3 and 4–4 defense. The purpose of this formation is to

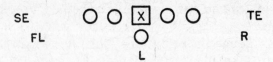

Figure 3.8 Double Twins Left.

throw quick passes into the flats and curl areas. This forces the
defense to drop their outside linebackers, giving the defense
additional pass support in the two under zones in the flats.
When this is done, run support by the defense becomes less
effective and the ground game with the solo halfback opens up.

Against the 4–4 defense, with their three-man secondary,
you may not want to run the ball at all. With an overload on both
sides of the formation, the three defensive backs cannot handle
the four wide receivers. This formation reduces the amount of
blitzing coming from outside linebackers. If the defense is
stubborn and continues to blitz from the outside, you can move
the ball with quick passes or quick screens to either side with
the slot halfback and flanker.

There is one major disadvantage to this formation. By
spreading your receivers wide, the two inside linebackers in
the 4–4 are able to blitz without worrying about inside zone
pass responsibilities. To counter this, the offense uses a combination of the double slot and double twins. One side of the
formation uses the slot, and the other side uses the twins. The
slot side can bring the slot man in tight to play the role of a tight
end. This receiver shores up additional blocking for running
plays and puts himself into a position where he can catch the
quick pass over the middle. Figures 3.9 and 3.10 illustrate
combinations of these two formations. The formations are
called as they are used in game situations.

By using combinations of the double twins and double slot
and moving one of the receivers in tight, you can dictate the
positioning of any or all the linebackers. The three-man secondary is not enough to cover the four receivers entering the
passing zones. Running the ball from these formations allows
the offense to hit the line quickly and effectively with dive and
slant plays. With linebacker coverage spread out, the offensive
line has the advantage by using false splits to set up necessary

blocking. By moving the tight slot in, he becomes an additional blocker who is also able to execute patterns over the middle, drag behind the tight end on a loop pattern, or be used as a ball carrier for an inside counter.

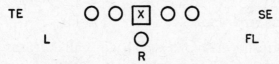

Figure 3.9   Twins Right, Slot Left.

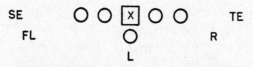

Figure 3.10   Twins Left, Slot Right.

The Pro Slot Combination

Like the double slot and double twins, the pro-T and slot formation can be used in combination. With the positioning of the slot man, there will be two outside and two inside receivers. This formation is used against all basic defenses and is extremely effective for both passing and running. As in all formations, the pro side is called first.

The pro-right slot-left formation places the tight end and flanker on the right side and the split end and left halfback on the left. The pro-left slot-right formation spots the tight end and flanker on the left and split end and right halfback to the right.

Normal splits should be used with this formation. False splits can be incorporated as the game progresses. Figures 3.11 and 3.12 show the combinations available and the terminology identifying each formation.

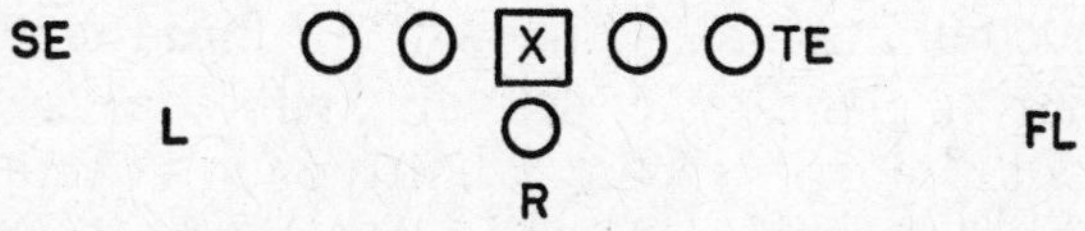

SE   ○ ○ ⊠ ○ ○TE

  L   ○   FL

             R

Figure 3.11   Pro Right, Slot Left.

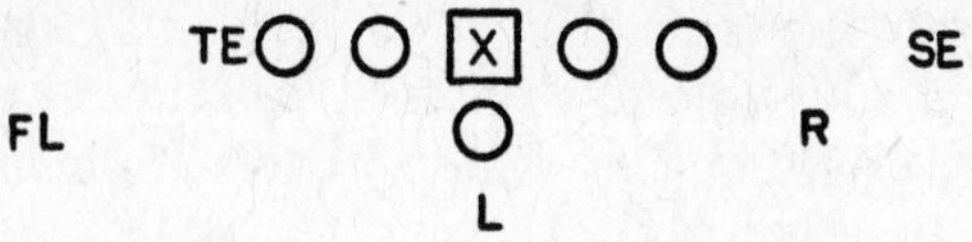

TE⭕ ⭕ ☒ ⭕ ⭕   SE
FL   ⭕   R
                     L

Figure 3.12   Pro Left, Slot Right.

The Trips Formation

The trips formation is used against all defenses. It is without a doubt one of the most difficult offensive alignments to defend. This formation relies on the overload principle. The trips positions three receivers on one side of the formation and the tight end on the other side. In the trips formation, the split end is always the widest receiver. The flanker is 1 yard off the line and approximately 4 yards in from the split end. Depending on which side this formation is called, one of the two halfbacks is the closest receiver and is positioned approximately 4 yards in from the flanker (see Figures 3.13 and 3.14).

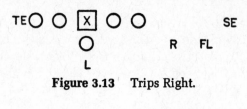

TE⭕ ⭕ ☒ ⭕ ⭕   SE
         ⭕   R   FL
         L

Figure 3.13   Trips Right.

SE   ⭕ ⭕ ☒ ⭕ ⭕TE
    FL   L   ⭕
                    R

Figure 3.14   Trips Left.

Although the defensive overload alignment remains consistent throughout our conference, different teams use each member of the overload differently. Depending on the team you are playing against, you may see a strict zone, strict man-to-man, or a combination of the two. All these defensive alternatives can be handled effectively with the use of motion. Motion tells the quarterback what type of coverage is being used. If the defense is playing in a man-to-man, one of the defensive backs leaves his original position in order to follow motion. If the defense is in a zone, the rotation goes in the direction of the motion man. In this case, the corner to the motion side slides out as the motion man moves his way.

To set up the deep pass the quarterback gives the tight end the option of executing a post or corner pattern. The tight end's key is the defensive corner to his side. If the corner moves out to cover the motion man, the tight end knows that a zone is being played. This tells him that he is to execute a deep corner pattern as quickly as possible so that he outruns the rotation of the middle safety (see Figure 3.15).

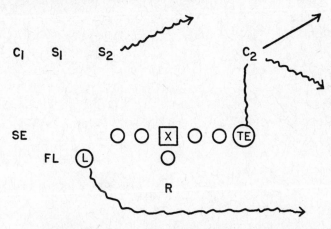

Figure 3.15   Reading the Defensive Secondary.

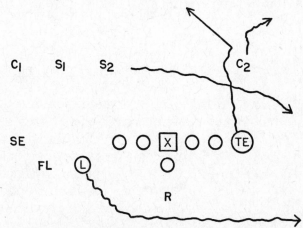

Figure 3.16   Reads Vs. Man-to-Man Coverage.

Eventually the defense realizes that a zone coverage will not be effective against the trips set with motion. The quarterback sees the coverage change when the safety follows the motion man across the entire formation. At this time, the tight ends read changes to the safety position. Looking for the corner pattern, the defensive corner (C_2) plays the tight end outside. As the tight end releases off the line he starts towards the corner as done previously. Then he changes his cut and turns towards the post. Since the safety has overlapped his man-to-man coverage, the middle one-third is left undefended (see Figure 3.16).

As the passing game becomes more effective, the pressure from the linebackers is restricted to pass defense. The trips formation allows the offense too many advantages for the linebackers to play stunting games. With additional run support

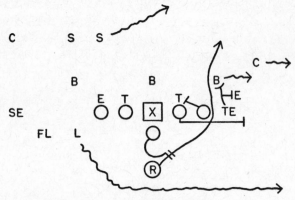

Figure 3.17   Trips Left, L-Even, 34 Dive.

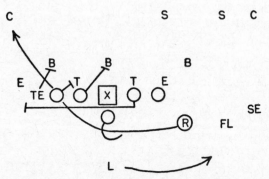

Figure 3.18   Trips Right, 35 Counter.

taken away, the running game becomes very effective. From the trips formation, there are many running plays that can be executed. Figures 3.17 and 3.18 are examples of two particular plays that are simple to execute and entirely effective.

The trips formation gives an offense that little extra needed to offset a more powerful and talented defense. An over-emphasis by the defense in trying to stop the pass opens up the ground game, and a more conservative defense trying to stop the run is eaten up through the air. This is one formation that puts the defense at a disadvantage no matter what they try to do.

Unbalanced Formation

The unbalanced formation is actually an offense in itself and forms the foundation for about 15 percent of all our running plays. Again, this formation can be used against all defenses. In the unbalanced formation, the tight end is positioned beside the offensive tackle on the weak side and the two guards, tackle, split end, and flanker are positioned on the opposite side (see Figures 3.19 and 3.20).

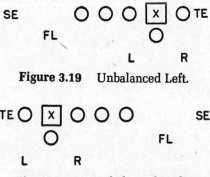

Figure 3.19   Unbalanced Left.

Figure 3.20   Unbalanced Right.

On the unbalanced side, the split end is out 10 to 12 yards and the flanker is positioned between 5 and 6 yards. The unbalanced formation forces the defense to shift before the snap. In many cases when this formation is applied and an off-tackle or sweep play is used, the defense cannot adjust quickly enough to counteract the angle blocking by the offensive line and receivers. This is a favorite formation used against 4—4 or split six defenses. Below are two different defenses we often see with this formation (see Figures 3.21 and 3.22).

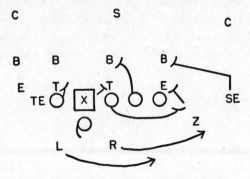

Figure 3.21　Angle Blocking Vs. Stack.

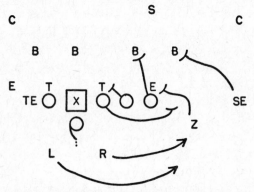

Figure 3.22　Angle Blocking Vs. Overshift.

In either case, angle blocking by the outside receivers and the offensive line can be used effectively. By shifting the backs to the left or right, either off-tackle play can be used success-fully. Counters with the flanker to the weak side can give this formation more offensive balance.

There is one more adjustment that can be made from this formation. The flanker can be positioned on the tight-end side as a set position, or he can be put there through the use of motion. In either case, the responsibility of the secondary changes drastically. There is one particular play that is used to work on the weak corner. As the play develops, the motion man tries to get as wide as possible before the snap. After the snap, the quarterback looks for two things. First, is the defensive corner moving out with the motion man? Second, where is the safety playing when motion is used? The defensive corner is in trouble no matter what he does. If the corner stays put and covers the tight end, the quarterback throws the ball to the motion man. If the corner slides out with motion, the tight end runs a deep corner pattern behind the defensive back (see Figure 3.23).

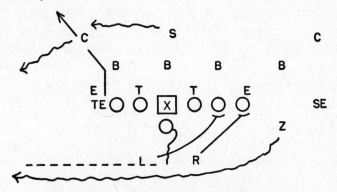

Figure 3.23   Motion Adjustment with Unbalanced Set.

By continually using this play, the safety has to help out the weak corner. As the safety moves over to cover the deep one-third to the outside, a very large area is left open for the opposite side corner to cover. Very few defensive backs have the ability to cover a split end man-for-man in an area this size (see Figure 3.24).

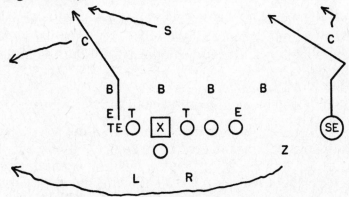

Figure   3.24   Motion   Adjustment   Used Against Overload by the Secondary.

All the formations mentioned in this chapter allow the offense to strike quickly and from any direction. The use of any one formation may not allow you to do what you would like offensively. By understanding the full potential of each formation and its function, you can choose the set that meets your needs in order to control the defense.

SPLITS USED IN THE PRO-T FORMATION

It is very important that the splits used by each member of the offensive team stay within the designated distance given by the offensive coaches. The distance between splits is determined by:

1. *The type of defense being played*

Certain defenses, such as the 52 and 43 rely on athletes who can read an offense and react to movement or keys. These defenses generally have excellent linebackers and linemen. Because of this, larger splits must be taken to spread out the defense. This allows the offensive blockers to use their quickness in creating a hole. In addition, by spreading the defense, larger holes will be created before the snap.

2. *The stunting ability of the defense*

The potential stunting ability of a defense can create numerous problems for an offensive line. When big splits are used, the defense has the edge. These large splits allow the linebackers to penetrate more rapidly. Tighter splits make up for poor blocking ability and compensate for the all-out defensive blitz.

3. *The defensive line adjustment to split changes*

A split change also changes the positioning of the defender. In high school, most defensemen are taught to line up on a specific individual. When playing against defensemen who move with the offensive man, a split change can be used to compensate for weak blocking up front (see False Splits).

4. *The nonadjusting stationary defender*

A defender often anchors himself in the same spot no matter what your splits are. The split may be extended a foot or two while the defender remains on your inside or outside shoulder. Numerous tricks can be played to pull the defender out of the play or set him up for trap blocking.

All of these adjustments aid offensive linemen in setting up the blocking scheme as a whole, or for one particular block.

Each member of the offensive line (including split and end flanker) is given a minimum and maximum distance to split in order to set up their blocking. To simplify this for the players, basic rules have been established.

1. Minimum splits are to be used against 62, 53, 44, and goal line defenses.
2. Maximum splits are used against 52, 43, and prevent types of defenses.

These particular rules are very important and should not be overlooked. As different defenses are used in practice, the linemen are expected to make mental adjustments on their own. With practice split changes become second nature. The basic splits used by each position are given in the table below.

	MAXIMUM	MINIMUM
Center	no splits allowed	
Guards	24 inches	18 inches
Tackles	36 inches	24 inches
Tight End	36 inches	24 inches
Flanker	12 yards	10 yards
Split End	12 yards	10 yards
Backs	2 yards from the heel of the quarterback to the front of their helmets (see Figure 3.25).	

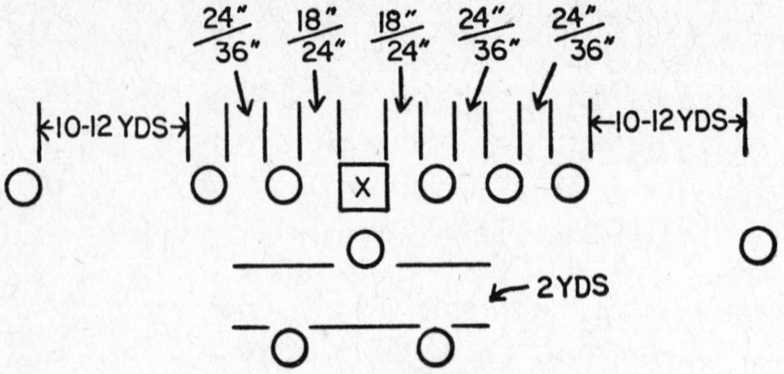

Figure 3.25   Normal Splits.

FALSE SPLITS

Split changes in the offensive line or receiver positions can be one of the best keys the defense has in reading a play. The defense sees the adjustment being made and may determine where the play is going.

The offense may use false splits to test the defense. These splits differ from the minimum and maximum split rules in that the splits can be reduced to 1 foot or widened up to 4 feet. Because football is becoming more of a game of thinking rather than brute force, these split changes are used for several reasons.

First, if an athlete is conditioned to respond automatically to a certain situation, he can be drawn away from a play or targeted for a future play. Second, in all 11 positions there is a one-on-one battle between the offense and the defense. One player may not be as well equipped physically as the other, so intelligence must be used as an equalizer. By changing to false splits, the blocker can move the defender into a position where he is better able to control him.

To test the defense, false splits are first used on the side of the formation away from the original play. Testing the defense by changing to false splits on the playside may become detrimental to the play.

Here is an example of the use of false splits. Run the ball to the right side of the formation. The left tackle and tight end on the opposite side use a false split of about 4 feet. If the two defenders are conditioned to play heads up or to the outside shoulder, as in the case of the defensive end, the defenders have taken themselves out of the play simply by following their normal alignment rules. This, in effect, can be used to set up the next play.

There is constant communication between the quarterback and his teammates. The left tackle may go back to the huddle and inform the quarterback that his hole is open for a play. The quarterback may decide to hit this hole on the next play or wait to see if the defense has seen the split change and adjusts accordingly. In the event that the next play called is through the tackle's hole, the blocking has been set as a result of the false split (see Figure 3.26).

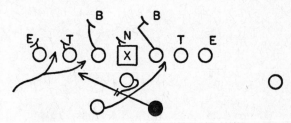

Figure 3.26   Use of False Splits to Set Up Plays.

False splits are extremely effective when used by the wide receivers. The false splits must be set up away from the play or during downs when running plays are being used. The receivers should not change their splits too drastically. Five-yard splits on one play and 15 on the next are too drastic. Splits should be changed very discreetly, 1 yard at a time. By doing this, the defensive back can be manipulated.

To illustrate this point, the split end is used as an example. His normal splits are 10 to 12 yards from the offensive tackle. If the corner is playing the receiver head up, the curl area between the defensive back and outside linebacker is difficult to penetrate (see Figure 3.27).

As the receiver cheats out, the corner moves with him. This opens up the curl area and cuts down the passing angle between the receiver and quarterback. Again, this split change must be set up 1 yard at a time (see Figure 3.28).

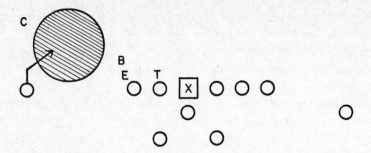

Figure 3.27   Normal Splits Vs. Open Zone.

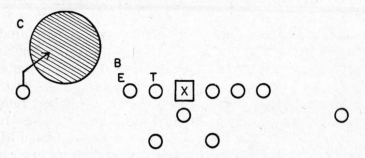

Figure 3.28   Open Zone Vs. False Splits.

False splits can give the offense one more weapon when dealing with a difficult defense. A smart athlete can totally control his opponent and make up for the physical difference which may exist.

BACKFIELD SETS

The pro-T attack uses three basic backfield sets. These sets can be used by one or both backs. Each set is used to overload or balance out the strength of the formation. The three backfield sets used are backs right, left, and normal. The backs right call is made by calling "rip." The right halfback lines up directly behind the right tackle and the left halfback positions himself directly behind the quarterback (see Figure 3.29).

The backs left call or liz, positions the left halfback behind the left tackle and the right halfback directly behind the quarterback (see Figure 3.30).

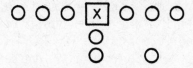

Figure 3.29   Backs Right (Rip).

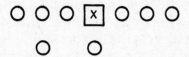

Figure 3.30   Backs Left (Liz).

There are many plays in which the backs are shifted. Looking at this from a defensive point of view, the defense may assume that the backs are shifted to add power to one specific side of the formation. This may cause the defense to shift the linebackers over to the strength of the backfield set, rather than the strength of the formation. This is often done when the backs are moved. The positioning of the linebackers has little or no effect on this shift. The pro-T often uses the shift to see how the defense adjusts or simply as a decoy for a passing play.

To show you the effects of the rip and liz calls, several plays will be discussed. One play that is extremely effective against the 43 defense is the straight dive up the middle with the right halfback. This formation is an overload to the left and looks like the typical off-tackle or power-sweep formation. In the huddle, the play is called: slot left—liz, 27 quick pitch action, 30 dive. This is a quick pitch fake to the left halfback, and then a dive by the right halfback through the center's hole.

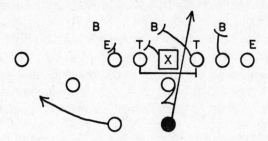

Figure 3.31   30 Dive from Liz Call.

If the linebackers are shifted over to their right, the play works and the right halfback is into the secondary before the safeties can realize it (see Figure 3.31).

When looking at this formation, one can see a possibility of the counterplay by the slot man. Blocking can be set up when the defense overshifts to the backfield strength.

By using the slot-left formation and shifting the backs to the right (rip call) another very successful play can be executed. It is very successful against the 62 and 52 defense. With the two linebackers in tight and a play-action dive from the left half-back, the counteroption play compensates for the defensive overshift (see Figure 3.32).

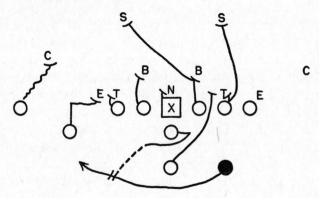

Figure 3.32   Slot Left—Rip, 20 Dive, 37 Option Pitch.

Shifting the backs helps set up passing plays. We will say that our scouting report informs us that the right defensive back rotates deep and quickly when the offensive play is run away from him. We set him up by using the pro-right formation with a rip call. The split end uses the false-split technique and keeps cheating in a couple of yards every play. To set this up either a sweep, off-tackle, or option play to the right is used several times. The split end during these plays performs a post pattern. When the time is right, an off-tackle play-action run is used, and the split end fakes the post and runs to the deep corner (see Figure 3.33).

For many years the wing-T offense has relied on misdirection and quick-hitting trap plays as a means of moving the

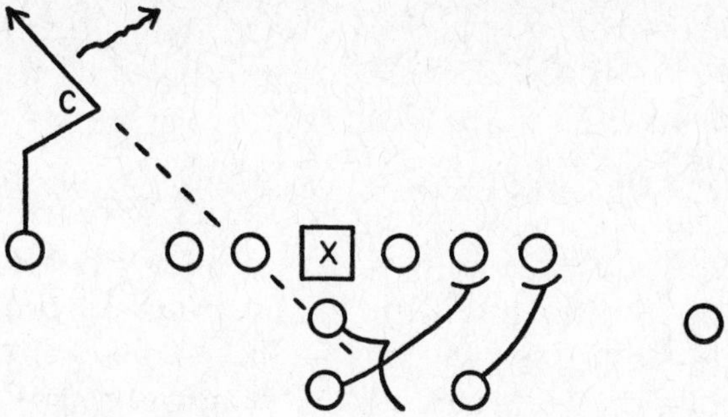

Figure 3.33   Rip Used to Influence the Defense.

football. The rip and liz calls have given the same effect with more versatility.

The split backs, or normal backfield position, puts the right halfback behind the right guard, and the left halfback behind the left guard. This adjustment is not called by the quarterback. If the liz and rip call is not made in the huddle the backs assume the normal split back's position.

Many of the formations used in the pro-T require a single back. The rip and liz calls also apply when one back is being used. The solo halfback always lines up directly behind the quarterback if no call is given.

HOLE NUMBERING

Each member of the offensive front line, including the outside receivers, is given a number. These numbers represent the specific hole where the play is to take place. The entire blocking scheme is based on a man-numbering system. This numbering system begins with the offensive center. He is identified with the number zero. The right side of the formation starts with the number 2 man who is the right guard, the tackle has the number 4 hole, and the outside receivers are identified with numbers 6 and 8. The left side starts with the number 1 man who is the offense left guard. The tackle is the number 3 man and the outside receivers are numbers 5 and 7. To show an example of this, the pro formation is used (see Figure 3.34).

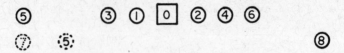

Figure 3.34   Hole-Numbering System.

You will note that there is no number 7 holeman. If the flanker was in the slot he would be the number 5 holeman and the split end would be the 7 holeman.

Below are several illustrations of various formations used in the pro-T attack. These formations are numbered according to the hole-numbering system (see Figures 3.35, 3.36, 3.37, and 3.38).

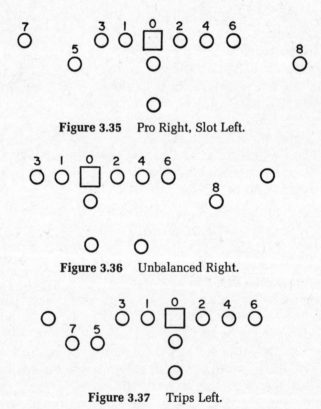

Figure 3.35   Pro Right, Slot Left.

Figure 3.36   Unbalanced Right.

Figure 3.37   Trips Left.

You will note that in the unbalanced right and trips left there is one member of the offensive line without a number.

Since all outside plays are called with 7 and 8 as a last digit, no other numbers are used.

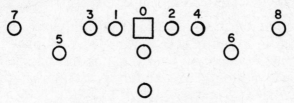

Figure 3.38   Double Slot Right.

BACKFIELD NUMBERING

Like the line, all backs are numbered. Their numbers remain the same no matter where they are positioned in the backfield. The quarterback is always number 1. The left back is number 2 and the right back is number 3. The flanker is used on many running plays. He is identified with the number 4 (see Figure 3.39).

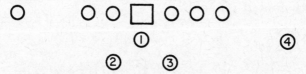

Figure 3.39   Backfield Numbering System.

When a formation is used that requires one of the backs to play in the slot position, he could be the holeman or ball carrier. When he is not involved directly in the play, he uses his hole number. If the slot man is the ball carrier, his backfield number is used (see Figure 3.40).

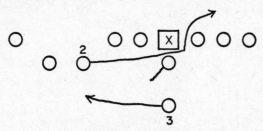

Figure 3.40   Trips Left, 22 Counter.

PLAY CALLING

In order to add new plays to this offense, there has to be a simple method of introducing and calling the plays. The quarterback is in control of the huddle, and any player who has information pertaining to blocking, possible pass patterns, or plays in general should inform the quarterback before the play is called.

In the pro-T attack all plays are called in this order:

1. Formation

Formation includes basic sets used. An example of this is as follows: pro-right, twins left, double slot right, etc. This also includes backfield direction rip and liz if needed.

2. Motion

Motion is always called second. If there is no motion being used, this step will be deleted.

3. The play, or action, used to set up the pass

On all plays, there is some kind of running action. When the play is strictly a running play the word *action* is deleted (example: 32 dive, 46 counter, 24 blast, etc.). In the event that a pass is thrown and the quarterback wants a running fake, the word *action* is added. This means that the play he calls uses that specific play fake (example: 32 dive action, 36 counteraction, 24 blast action, etc.).

4. Snap count

The quarterback calls the formation, motion (if needed), and the play or action. Then he informs the offense when the ball is to be snapped. An example of the play calling is as follows: trips left, Z-even, 33 dive action, 694 on two (with motion). Trip left, 33 dive action, 694 on two (without motion). The snap count is also given in order.

1. Ready: All offensive linemen make their blocking calls.
2. Set: All members of the offense get into the set position.
3. Color: There is a color given at the line of scrimmage on every play. If the live color for that particular game is called, the play that was called in the huddle is cancelled. The number that follows the live color informs the offense what play to execute.

To make these audibles simple to remember, seven plays are used. Each play has a specific number and is shown below.

1. Both backs dive through the guard holes.
2. Quick slant (pop) by the split end and flanker.
3. Quick pass to the tight end (Y-shoot).
4. Off-tackle power play to the right (24 blast).
5. Off-tackle power play to the left (35 blast).
6. Quarterback roll right—throw or run.
7. Quarterback roll left—throw or run.

The seven audible calls get the offense out of most situations. Linebacker blitzing can be effectively handled in the number 2 and number 3 play changes. The number 4 and number 5 take care of most inside pressure which may result with an anticipated quarterback sneak.

The audible change in number 6 and number 7 allows the quarterback to run or pass. With these options given to the quarterback, tremendous pressure can be put on the defensive secondary especially if they are in a six- or eight-man line.

An example of the play calling and audible system for a game in which the live color is black is shown. In both examples, the play in the huddle is given; Pro-right, 24 blast on two.

"Ready, set, blue 8, blue 8, hut! hut!"

In this case, the live color was not given. The original off-tackle blast is executed.

"Ready, set, black 6, black 6, hut! hut!"

In this case, the live color (black) has changed the play to a roll right by the quarterback with the option to run or pass.

Play Calling for Running Plays

In the pro-T attack all running backs, including the flanker, are given a number identifying them for running plays. The quarterback in this system is given the number 1. A typical running play for the quarterback is the quarterback draw. The play is called ten. This means the number 1 back is run through the 0 hole. The left halfback is given the number 2 and the right back is number 3 and the flanker is given the number 4. Don't let the letters L, R, and Z confuse you, as the letters are used on passing plays only. The flanker is identified with the number 4 in case he is called on to carry the ball.

Two numbers are given when calling the running plays. The first number represents the ball carrier and the second number tells the back which holeman to run behind. This is very basic in all offenses. As an example of this, the play slot left, 33 blast is used. This is an off-tackle play to the left side (see Figure 3.41).

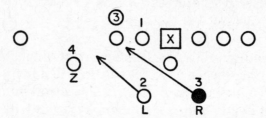

Figure 3.41   Number 3 Back Through the Number 3 Hole.

Play Calling for the Passing Game

The implementation of pass patterns requires a simple form of play calling. In the pass-calling phase of the pro-T attack, all patterns are called from left to right using the patterns illustrated in chapter 4.

The formations used or location of each receiver have no bearing on the patterns called. The primary receivers are those located on the line of scrimmage or 1 yard off. These receivers receive their routes first. The secondary or backfield receivers get their pattern second. To show an example of primary pattern called, the pro-right formation is used and the huddle call is pro right, 693 (see Figure 3.42).

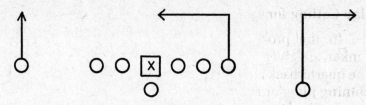

Figure 3.42 Pattern Called from Left to Right.

A more complicated play call involving four receivers is still called from left to right. We will incorporate several of the specific types of patterns mentioned in chapter 4 (see Figure 3.43).

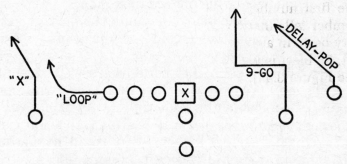

Figure 3.43 Pro Left, Slot Right, X, Loop, 9-Go, Delay-Pop.

Both of these examples show how the primary pass receivers' pass patterns are called. When incorporating the secondary receivers into this pattern, the code letters L and R are used. When combining the primary and secondary receivers into the

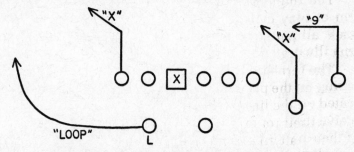

Figure 3.44 Use of Secondary Receiver in Loop Pattern.

pattern, first the primary receivers' patterns are given followed by the backfield patterns. An example of this is the unbalanced X, X, 9, L-loop (see Figure 3.44).

This system is simple and effective when calling pass patterns. No matter what formation is used, the patterns are always called from left to right with primary to secondary receivers called in order.

THE USE OF MOTION

Motion has added one more weapon to the explosiveness of this attack. The strength of a set can be changed simply by putting one member of the offense in motion.

Motion is performed by one of the potential receivers off the line of scrimmage. This includes all the primary receivers along with the halfbacks.

When calling motion, the quarterback uses the identification letter to inform a player that he will be used to run motion. Once this player is identified, the words *even* or *odd* will follow the code letter. If the even call is given to the motion man, he runs to the right side of the formation. If odd, he runs to the left. To show an example of this the trips formation is used, and the play is called: trips right, Z-odd, X, X, loop, fire (see Figure 3.45).

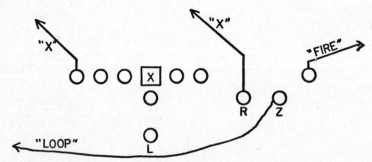

Figure 3.45   Flanker to Odd Side Executes Loop Pattern.

Motion is used to balance the formation by sending the motion man across the formation. Motion can also be used to move one receiver outside another. In this case, the flanker is in the slot and will be moving to the outside rather than the inside. The play called is: slot right, Z-even, 2, 3-go, 3 (see Figure 3.46).

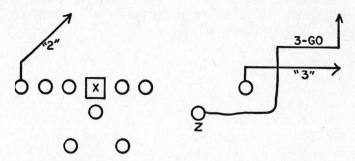

Figure 3.46   Motion Executes 3-Go to Even Side.

In both examples we have used the flanker to illustrate the use of motion. The left and right halfback can also be put in motion first by identifying them, and second, by giving the direction in which motion is to be used. A typical example in which we use motion is against a linebacker who is playing outside of the defensive end in an Okie Eagle adjustment. Motion by the left halfback may draw the linebacker's attention, and he may decide to move out with the back. This opens up the off-tackle hole for the right halfback. It also opens up the short hook and curl zones for the split end on a slant pattern. An example of this is the call: slot left, L-odd, pop, 7, 0 (see Figure 3.47).

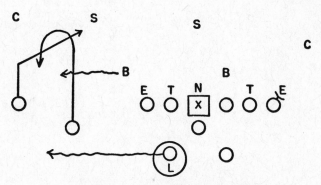

Figure 3.47   Halfback Odd Motion.

Motion Involvement in the Pattern

Before the motion man moves, he is in the set position. When the pass patterns are called in the huddle, the motion man is given his pattern according to where he is in the left-to-right relationship. To show this the play is: twins left, Z-even, 6, 2, 5 (see Figure 3.48).

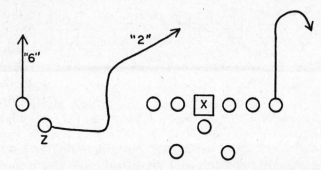

Figure 3.48   Motion Executes 2 Pattern.

As the play is called, the flanker or motion man is the second receiver from the left and the 6 25 lets the split end know he will run the 6 pattern. The motion man starts in motion and on the snap turns upfield and runs a 2 pattern. The tight end does a 5 pattern. The motion patterns used by all receivers can have additional patterns added to them once the ball has been snapped. A very popular pattern used by the back is the 5 and 7 patterns from motion. To illustrate this, the play called is: twins left, liz, L-odd, 5X05 (see Figure 3.49).

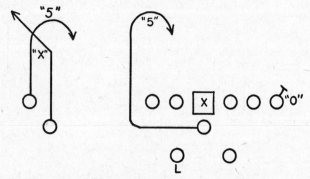

Figure 3.49   Halfback Motion in 5 Pattern.

Since the 5 pattern was given last in the pass pattern call, the left halfback does a 5 pattern.

Isolation Patterns with Motion

Within the pro-T attack, motion can be used to isolate one specific receiver. By isolating this receiver, we can use him for a quick screen pass. The flanker and left and right halfbacks are generally used to run the isolation patterns. As the isolation receiver is running motion, he tries to go behind the receiver or group of receivers prior to the snap. After the snap, the quarterback fakes a dive to the side away from motion. Then he pivots in the direction of motion and rifles the ball to the motion receiver. Below are three examples of how the motion man can be used in an isolation pattern (see Figures 3.50, 3.51, and 3.52).

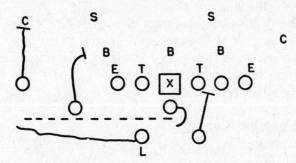

Figure 3.50   Slot Left, L-Odd, L-Quick Screen.

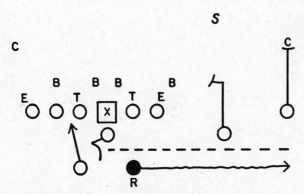

Figure 3.51   Slot Right, R-Even, R-Quick Screen.

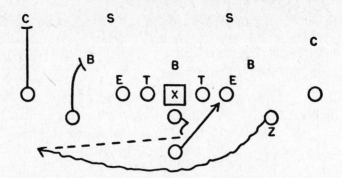

Figure 3.52 Double Slot Right, Z-Odd, Z-Quick Screen.

Using the isolation receiver, the quarterback must always look deep or in another direction before turning back and throwing to the motion man.

In the quick screen series, the outside receivers must go downfield and block the closest defender to the play. Because of the quickness with which this play takes place, the outside receivers can break from the line of scrimmage and start their block immediately.

Motion Used for Blocking

Certain formations within the pro-T attack require additional blocking from the motion receiver. When the motion man is brought into a play to block, he is given the 0 pattern.

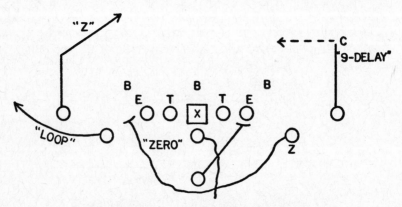

Figure 3.53 Flanker Used as Blocker.

This informs the motion man that he is responsible for blocking the motion side pass rush. To show an example of this, the play double slot right, Z-odd, 2, loop, 0, 9-delay is called (see Figure 3.53).

The plays and description of terminology in this chapter have given you a basic idea of how this offense can be used to attack certain defensive adjustments. Only a few examples have been given to show how each pattern is used. This basic passing system gives you the ability to work on any defense with success simply by making the defense do what you want them to do.

HUDDLE PROCEDURE

The huddle is positioned 10 yards from the line of scrimmage. After the play has been called, the center and all wide receivers, including the halfbacks if they are in a spread formation, break from the huddle. The play is repeated by the quarterback, and the huddle will break with, "Ready" . . . "Break!" (see Figure 3.54).

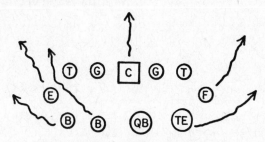

Figure 3.54   Huddle Positioning.

4

UNDERSTANDING THE PRO-T PASSING TERMINOLOGY

Because of the versatility of this offense, there has to be a system that covers all facets of the passing attack and yet remains simple enough to understand. This chapter deals with the terminology used in the passing game. It includes all pass patterns and their use in the passing game. Specific coaching tips are given throughout this chapter in order to help the receiver who is not gifted with speed or quickness.

TERMINOLOGY

In the pro-T passing attack, all potential pass receivers are identified with a letter. These letters are used to single out each receiver and remain with the receiver no matter which formation is used. Players in the offensive line are also designated with a specific letter.

The split end is always identified by the letter X or symbol ($\otimes$). The tight end is the letter Y or ($\square$), and the flanker is identified with the letter Z or symbol ($\odot$).

Many pass patterns are executed with the use of the two halfbacks. To make this simple to remember, the left halfback is given the letter L or symbol ($\oslash$), and the right halfback becomes R or symbol ($\ominus$). The quarterback is not used for any type of throwback passing or trick plays. He is much too important to this offense to be used as a receiver. The quarterback may be identified with the letter Q or symbol (◬) (see Figure 4.1).

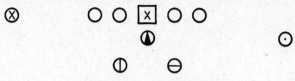

Figure 4.1   Pro Right.

PASS PATTERNS

We have used many systems or gimmicks in teaching pass patterns and have found one that works extremely well. This pro-T pass system consists of ten basic pass patterns which are used as base patterns. The clock face has been incorporated into this system as a means of teaching the patterns. All pass patterns are called by using either single-digit numbers or single words. Since the clock has numbers with double-digit figures (10, 11, 12) these numbers had to be replaced by changing the 10 and 11 to the letter X and the number 12 with the number 6. Normally the number 6 is at the bottom of the clock, therefore, this number had to be replaced with the number 0. When the number 0 is called, the pass receiver is used as a pass blocker rather than a receiver (see Figure 4.2).

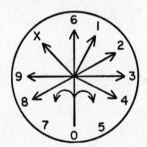

Figure 4.2   Base Pass Patterns.

In running these patterns, all receivers start at the 0 position or line of scrimmage. On the snap, the receiver runs approximately 10 yards downfield and makes his break to the number on the clock. As an example, the pro-T formation is used. The split end runs an X pattern, the tight end executes the 3 pattern, and the flanker runs a 2 pattern (see Figure 4.3).

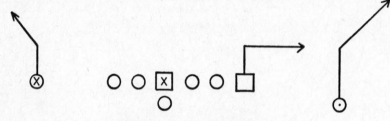

Figure 4.3   Pro Right, X32.

This method of calling the pass patterns has proven to be extremely effective in the area of remembering the various patterns. It is simple and yet gives a minimum of ten basic patterns which can be used. The 10-yard distance that the receiver runs before making his cuts varies. This will be covered later in the chapter.

GO ADJUSTMENT

In order to add a new wrinkle to the base patterns, the word *go* is added to each number. When *go* is added to the base pattern, the receiver runs the base pattern and then adds a 90 degree cut off the base pattern upfield or to the sidelines. All patterns use the go adjustment with the exception of the 6 and 0 patterns.

In calling these patterns, the base pattern is always given first. The word *go* follows the base pattern. An example of this would be the 5-go, 4-go, 9-go, etc. The Z-out pattern in the pro-T attack is the X-go or 2-go, depending on which side of the formation the receiver is on. The 3-go and 9-go take the place of the down out and down (see Figure 4.4).

By incorporating the ten base patterns with the addition of the go adjustment, you will have a full complement of pass patterns. As mentioned before, the distance at which the cuts are made will vary. To say that each pattern should be run at approximately 10 yards downfield before the cut is made, is not taking into account actual playing conditions. Different types of defenses allow more flexibility than others, and for this reason all receivers are instructed on the techniques used to read the secondary.

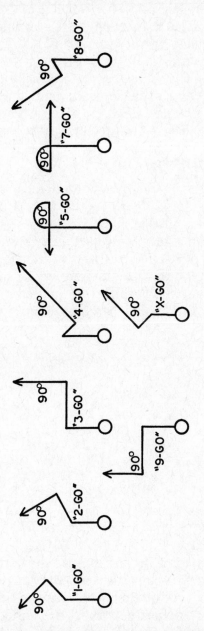

Figure 4.4   Base Patterns with the Go Adjustment.

CUTS AGAINST THE ZONE COVERAGE

All defenders in the zone coverage are basically the same as outfielders in baseball. When a ball is hit to the outfield, the longer the ball remains in the air the easier it becomes to catch. This principle also applies to pass plays. This is one major reason why coaches may not wish to give their receivers a certain distance they must run before making their cuts. The receivers are taught to make basic reads that will help them determine the distance at which their cuts are to be made.

There are two basic things that the receivers must look for.

1. *Rotation of the zone*

All wide receivers key on the defensive corner to their side. This corner either supports the flats area, or moves back into the deep one-third and lets the safety on his side move up into the flats. Since the receivers already know where the play action is taking place, they will know where the rotation will be before the snap. To further illustrate this, a 2 pattern is run by the split end. The action used by the quarterback is an off-tackle play to the split-end side (see Figure 4.5).

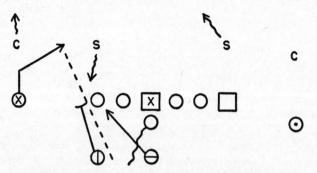

Figure 4.5   Early Cut Vs. Safety Rotation.

In this case, the split end makes his cut at 5 to 7 yards. He makes his cut early because the secondary has reacted to the run and is not in a deep rotation. The split end must try to hit the seam between the defensive corner on his side and the safety on the opposite side.

2. Initial movement of the corner

The defensive coverage can also be used as a key. Once the corner commits himself and comes up into the flats area, the receiver knows that the safety to his side is moving into the deep third zone. This informs the receiver that he can run deeper before making his cut. Since the rotation is moving to the split-end side, the strong safety moves deep and toward the split end. The post, or 2 pattern, is run deeper and under the coverage of the free safety. In this instance, the receiver makes his cut at 10 to 12 yards (see Figure 4.6). In both examples the rotation moves in the direction of the play-action side.

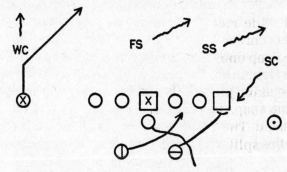

Figure 4.6 Late Cut Vs. Secondary Rotation Away.

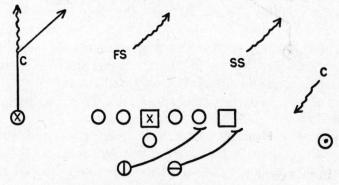

Figure 4.7 Cuts Vs. Rotation Away.

When action is run away from the receiver, all patterns can be run deeper. The weak corner moves away into his deep third coverage, while both the free safety and strong safety rotate deep and away from the split end. This opens up a seam between the weak corner and free safety and enables the receiver to run deeper before his initial cut is made (see Figure 4.7).

CUTS VERSUS MAN-TO-MAN COVERAGE

When facing a man-to-man secondary coverage, the distance at which the cuts are made is second in priority to the cuts themselves. When playing against man-to-man coverages, the receivers are taught to stay as far away from the defensive backs as possible when running their patterns. Although there is no rotation in this type of defense, the receivers still key their respective opponent.

An obvious key that helps the receiver is the depth at which the defenders are playing. Defensive backs who have above-average to good skills generally play the receivers tight by using a 5 to 7 yard cushion. This type of defender is confident in his ability and is generally harder to fake out of position. The less experienced defender gives up a bigger cushion and hopes that the distance between himself and the receiver will make up for the lack of experience in covering a deep pattern. A general rule for receivers is: The deeper the cushion a defender uses, the more quickly the receiver's cuts must be made, and the tighter the cushion a defender uses, the deeper the receiver's cuts must be made.

When playing against the man-to-man defense, the go adjustments, or picks, are used rather than the base patterns. The second cut, or go cut, is affected greatly by the depth of the cushion given up by the defensive backs. To show this, an X pattern with the go adjustment is illustrated.

The corner who gives up the big cushion has to be turned out of position in order for the receiver to get open quickly. The split end runs his base pattern at about 5 yards. He makes his first cut off the X pattern. After running about 5 more yards, he breaks to the post and completes his X-go pattern. Running a longer distance on his first cut is unnecessary because the defensive corner is already 10 to 12 yards away. The receiver must get open as quickly as possible so the ball can be thrown over the linebacker coverage (see Figure 4.8).

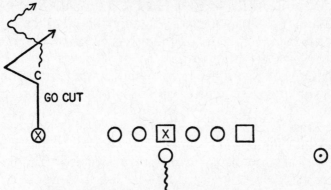

GO CUT

Figure 4.8   X-Go Pattern Vs. Deep Cushion.

The more experienced defensive back plays the receiver much tighter. This requires the receiver to run his first cut deeper in order to take the corner further out of position before the go cut is made. As the receiver breaks off the line, he runs approximately 10 to 12 yards in the direction of the defensive corner. As he is making his first out cut he should accelerate, forcing the defender to start running stride-for-stride with him. When the receiver is sure that the defender is covering him on the corner pattern, he heads to the post and continues running his X-go pattern. At this time, the defender should have been turned around and unable to cover the receiver tightly (see Figure 4.9).

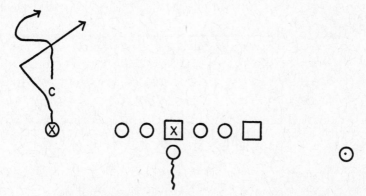

Figure 4.9   X-Go Pattern Vs. Tight Cushion.

QUICK PATTERNS: FIRE-GO-POP

The quick series involves patterns that are executed immediately. These patterns are the quick slant, quick out, and quick pass to the tight end. To identify these patterns, words are used in place of a numbering system. These patterns are the base patterns quick series, and all words used to describe these patterns are common words which the players can relate to.

A common phrase used in football is "fire out." By combining these two words the receiver can relate the word *fire* with the quick out pattern. The fire is executed by taking 2 steps off the line of scrimmage and cutting at a 90 degree angle to the sideline. A 45 degree cut may be used if the quarterback and receiver work on the spot-passing theory. In spot passing, the quarterback throws the ball to a specific spot or target and the receiver adjusts his pattern so that he can get to the designated target. Figure 4.10 is an illustration of the fire pattern using a go cut. Figure 4.11 illustrates the fire call with a spot passing

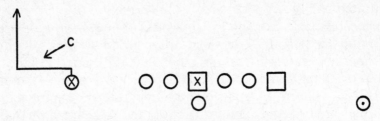

Figure 4.10   Split End Using the X-Fire Pattern with a Go Cut.

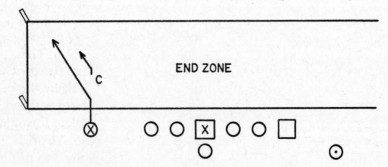

Figure 4.11   Split End Using the X-Fire Pattern with Spot Passing.

adjustment. The spot used by the quarterback and receiver is the pylon in the corner of the end zone.

As in all cases of the quick series, the quarterback fakes a dive to the playside halfback, takes one step back, plants, and throws.

The phrase "shoot-straight" is also used as a teaching aid and can make the pattern easily understood by the receivers. The shoot pattern is a quick 6 pattern. This pass is generally thrown to the tight end but can also be used effectively by the outside receivers. When the tight end runs this pattern, he takes one step from the line of scrimmage and immediately looks for the ball. To set this pass up, an off-tackle type of play action is used. When the outside linebacker is supporting the off-tackle action, he is not in position to prevent the tight end from clearing the line of scrimmage (see Figure 4.12).

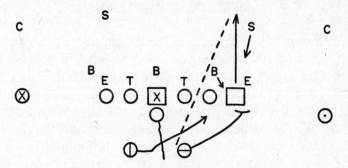

Figure 4.12   Shoot Pattern to Tight End.

The pop pattern is nothing more than a quick inside slant. When executing this pattern, the receiver takes two driving, aggressive steps off the line of scrimmage. Then he breaks at a 45 degree angle towards the middle of the formation. This type of play works very effectively against defenses that use the Okie Eagle adjustment by the outside linebackers. To draw the linebacker out of position, motion can be used by either the halfback or flanker. To illustrate this in its simplest form, motion comes from the right halfback to the playside. An off-tackle action from the left halfback to the right side is used to pick up the defensive end. This action causes the outside linebacker to move out with the motion man and support the off-tackle play.

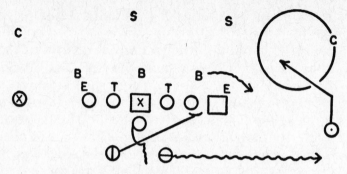

Figure 4.13 Flanker Runs Pop Pattern.

Again, the quarterback fakes to the slant back, sets, and throws (see Figure 4.13).

ISOLATION PATTERNS

The pop-fire and shoot patterns are part of the isolation series. This series concentrates on one specific receiver. Because of the time factor involved, the quarterback doesn't have time to look for all the receivers. When calling these plays, the identification letters are used. In the huddle, the quarterback calls the formation and gives the code letter and the pattern to be executed. Here is an example of an isolation play called: slot left, Z-even, 33 blast, (motion by flanker to right side of the formation) X-pop (see Figure 4.14). As you can see, play action is again performed on the playside.

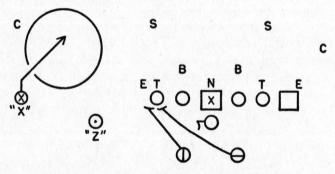

Figure 4.14 Isolation X-Pop Pattern by the Split End.

The isolation series of plays attempts to manipulate one specific defensive position. Scouting reports reveal on which linebacker to use them. When using these patterns, the quarterback reads the linebacker to the playside. The linebacker's actions tell the quarterback when and where he is to throw. An aggressive linebacker has the tendency to support the run and not worry about the quick slant. An inexperienced player may not move in either direction because of his uncertainty in locating the ball. It is much easier to read the aggressive player than it is to read the player who lacks experience. When facing the aggressive defender, the pass can be delayed allowing the receiver more time to clear the line of scrimmage and find a bigger opening in the linebacker zone. Caution must be taken, however, against waiting too long so that the slant receiver runs into the overlapping zone coverage of the middle or inside line-

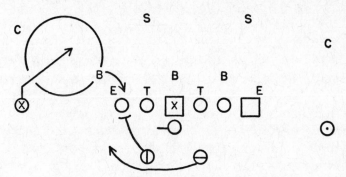

Figure 4.15   X-Pop Vs. Aggressive Linebacker.

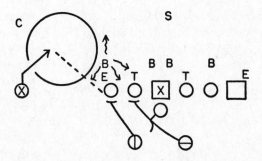

Figure 4.16   X-Pop Vs. the Inexperienced Linebacker.

backer. This could result in an interception. When throwing this pass against the inexperienced linebacker, the receiver should look for the ball early. This gives him time to tuck the ball away and start his open field maneuvers (see Figures 4.15 and 4.16).

The isolation patterns prevent linebacker blitzing from becoming a problem. In the event that a blitz is read by the quarterback, he simply uses a live color to audible a quick pattern into the area of the blitzing linebacker.

READ CALLS

The read call is also incorporated into the isolation series. Like all isolation patterns, the quarterback notifies one specific receiver that he is the primary target. The read call is generally used inside the opponent's 10-yard line. Quick patterns are more effective when the read call is used, and the chance of an interception is minimized.

When inside the 10-yard line, most defensive backs position themselves so that they give up the inside or outside pattern to the receiver. From the defensive standpoint, the defensive backs are able to force the receiver to the inside or outside by positioning themselves where they don't want the receiver to go. If a play is called in the huddle and the defensive back has guessed the play correctly, chances of the pass being completed are slim.

The read call is coordinated between the isolation receiver and the quarterback. Both the receiver and quarterback watch the defender to the playside and determine whether he is playing the receiver to the outside or inside. If the corner is playing to the receiver's inside, both the receiver and quarterback know that the isolation series will be executed using outside patterns. These patterns could be a fire, square out, or corner. In any case, this is a quick passing play and the receiver must take two steps before making his cut. We do not encourage a fake by the receiver in order to set up his determined pattern. This takes too long, and the receiver may not turn around soon enough to get a good view of the pass. As an example of this, the quarterback calls, "Z-read." In this case, the flanker is the primary receiver (see Figure 4.17).

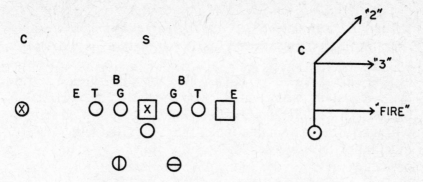

Figure 4.17   Z-Read Vs. Inside Coverage.

An experienced defensive back takes away the outside and relies on inside help from either the linebacker or strong safety. This adjustment takes away the outside read. At this point, the primary goal is to try to get the safety to move out of his position and help support the run in order to open up the slant pattern for the receiver. When running this play against the four-deep zone, a sweep action is used to the isolation receiver's side. We know that the defensive corner does not leave the seam uncovered in order to stop this play, so the safety is the only one who is supporting from the outside. As the safety moves out of position to come up on the sweep action, the quarterback and receiver read this accordingly, and the ball is thrown. The quarterback reverses, pivots, and fakes the handoff to the sweep back, turns, plants, and throws (see Figure 4.18).

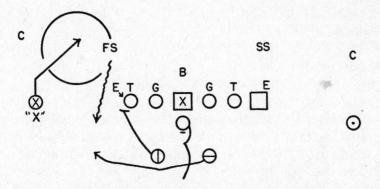

Figure 4.18   X-Read Vs. Outside Coverage.

Motion used near the goal line can change secondary responsibilities drastically, especially when the defense is playing man-to-man. Because of this, a combination of two or three receivers may be given the read call. This is an easy read for the quarterback since he can see the defense adjust to the motion man. The outside receivers rely on the inside or outside relationship of the defender in order to determine the patterns they will use. When a combination of reads is called, cross buck or dive action is used. This action ties up the linebackers and prevents them from dropping into their zones before the pass is thrown (see Figure 4.19).

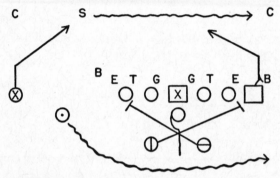

Figure 4.19   X-Read and Y-Read Vs. the Gap 8
Defense.

From this illustration, you can see that the motion man created a rotation by the safety. This opened up the post pattern for both the split end and tight end. The read call series has scored more touchdowns than any other single play used in this offense. Its effectiveness cannot be doubted, and it is extremely tough to stop because defenses are unable to guess where the pattern will be executed.

DELAY PATTERNS

The delay patterns are used to bring one receiver into an area that has been cleared out by another receiver. The delay call is added at the end of the base call. An example of this would be the 3-delay.

When using delay patterns, the receiver breaks from the line of scrimmage to a distance of 10 yards. He pauses for one full second and continues to run the base pattern called. The delay patterns give the receiver an opportunity to find his own hole in the secondary coverage, rather than running one specific pattern and going with the do or die philosophy. This pattern also acts as a safety valve for the quarterback in case he is driven out of the pocket or can't find a deep receiver open (see Figure 4.20).

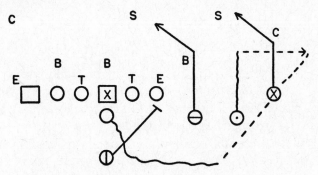

Figure 4.20   The Flanker Runs a 3-Delay Pattern (Z-3 Delay).

The delay call may also be incorporated with the quick series pass patterns. When using a combination of the delay and quick series patterns, the word *delay* comes in front of the quick pattern. In this case, the receiver delays his start from the line of scrimmage for one count and then continues to run the pattern called. When this delay pattern is used, the receiver is identified with his code letter. This helps clear up the confusion between the 3-delay, 6 and the 3, delay-6. The trips left formation is used as an example of how the patterns are given, and how the use of the code letter simplifies and clarifies the difference between the delay on the line of scrimmage and the delay downfield (see Figure 4.21). The call for this pattern would be: trips left, 2, 5, L-delay, fire, 0.

The letter L isolates the left halfback as the delay receiver and he remains in his position for 1 second before running the pattern given to him by the quarterback. When using a pattern

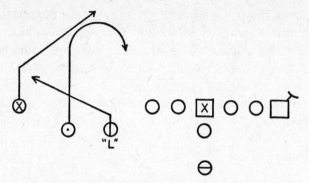

Figure 4.21   L-Receiver Runs a Delay-Fire
Pattern.

of this type, it is important that the quarterback looks away from
the delay man. The quarterback does not want any more attention brought to the delay receiver than is necessary. By looking
away, the quarterback gives the delay receiver time to sneak
into an unoccupied defensive area. This also gives the receiver
time to set up so that he is in a better position to catch and run.

PICKS

The pick patterns are specifically used to detour one of the
defensive backs from covering a receiver. The technique used is
very similar to the pick in basketball, however, the receivers
never attempt to make contact with the defender in order to free
up another receiver.

The pick can be run by any receiver and the combination of
patterns used may vary according to the situation. To illustrate
this, the slot formation is used. The split end runs a pick 5 and
the slot man executes an X pattern. When the split end breaks
from the line of scrimmage, he runs as tightly as possible to the
defensive corner. When the split end is within two or three
steps from the corner, he turns to the inside and executes the 5
pattern. The flanker follows behind the split end until he sees
the split end plant, and starts to turn to his inside. Then the slot
receiver runs as tightly as possible to the split end before making his X cut. By doing this, the receivers are attempting to
freeze the defensive corner on the split end and prevent him

from picking up the slot receiver. Again we emphasize the fact that the split end should not try to make physical contact with the defensive corner. The split end simply provides a curtain to obstruct the view of the corner (see Figure 4.22).

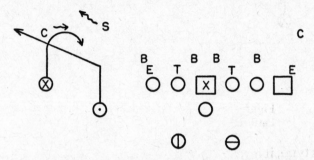

Figure 4.22 Pick Pattern Used by the Split End Vs. Man-to-Man Coverage.

When using the pick series, the offense continues to use this particular pattern until the defense makes some kind of adjustment. Basically there are three types of defensive changes.

1. To stop this play, an outside linebacker is positioned into the hook or curl area in order to give added support, for the defensing of the 5 pattern (inside curl). By doing this, the two remaining defensive backs can cover the flanker if he runs a post or corner pattern. When this adjustment is made by the defense, the pick series is reversed and a go adjustment is added. In this case, the split end runs a 2 pattern and the flanker executes a pick 7-go (see Figure 4.23).

   As the linebacker is pulled from his normal position, he leaves a vacant area between himself and the inside linebackers. This is a big area and can be further opened by the 2 pattern used by the split end. The safety in this case cannot support the curl because he has man-to-man responsibilities with the split end. The defensive corner cannot help the linebacker because he is unaware of the direction in which the split end will break, and he cannot give up the outside one-third. In the event that the corner does help the linebacker, the split end could run a 2-go pattern.

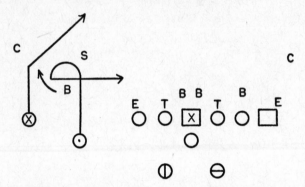

Figure 4.23   Pick Pattern Vs. Outside Linebacker Support.

2. The second defensive adjustment commonly used is the switch call made by the secondary. This is nothing more than a zone coverage between the corner and safety. Whichever receiver breaks into his zone is his responsibility. In order to take advantage of this, the receivers flood the outside zone with a deep pattern and the inside zone with a short pattern. The defensive man cannot cover both receivers and will most likely pick up the deep threat.

   This adjustment can be altered by running one pattern and switching receiver assignments. In the slot, the split end runs a 7 pattern or outside curl, and the flanker executes an X pattern (see Figure 4.24).

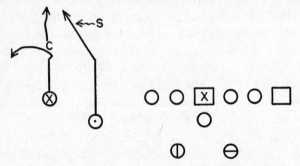

Figure 4.24   Pick Adjustment Vs. Zone Coverage.

The results are the same by having the split end run an X pattern and the flanker a 7 pattern. This change forces the defensive corner deep right away because he clearly sees that the split end has moved deep on his pattern. The flanker may also free himself up a bit since the safety is backpedalling deep, as the flanker is curling towards the sideline (see Figure 4.25).

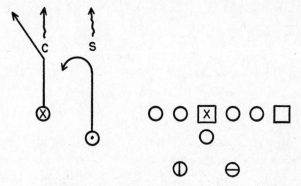

Figure 4.25 Pick Adjustment Vs. Zone Coverage—Reverse Patterns.

3. The third adjustment is the staggered or monster coverage. This defensive adjustment puts one defender in the short under zone, and one in the deep third. This alternative is generally seen against the four-deep secondary, which does not use linebacker support in the flats area. When the staggered coverage is used, the quarterback is able to see the rotation and the depth at which all members of the secondary are playing. He sees that one corner is supporting the flats to the slant side and the other three defensive backs are covering the deep thirds. To compensate for this, both receivers are sent into the middle area that is covered by the safety.

To show an example of this, the slot man or flanker executes a 2 pattern and chases the safety into the deep third. The split end runs a 2-delay pattern. As the split end breaks from the line of scrimmage he comes up to the corner, pauses for a second, and continues his 2 pattern. By the time the split end gets into the middle third, the safety has been cleared out (see Figure 4.26).

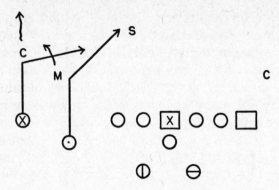

Figure 4.26 Picks Used Against Staggered (Monster) Coverage.

THE LOOP SERIES

Like the pick series, the loop series is basically used against the man-to-man and three-deep zone coverages. This particular series is one of the toughest to defend against because the secondary is not in position to stop this play.

When performing loop patterns, the receiver runs directly behind and outside of the outside receiver in the formation. As the ball is snapped, the loop receiver literally runs along the line of scrimmage. Once he is outside of the outside receiver, he turns upfield and runs at a 45 degree angle towards the sideline. This takes him out of the range of the safety (see Figure 4.27).

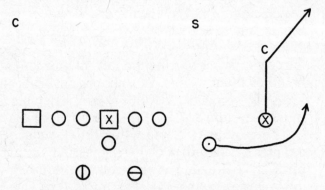

Figure 4.27 Flanker Runs Loop Pattern Vs. 3-Deep Zone Coverage.

When running the loop against the three-deep zone coverage, the outside receiver should run a pattern that forces the defensive corner into the deep third area to his side. This neutralizes his effectiveness in covering the loop receiver.

When used against strict man-to-man secondary coverages, the safety is not able to stop the loop receiver from getting open. He has to start moving over as soon as he sees the loop receiver begin his pattern. The quarterback continues to call this pattern until the safety has started moving to the outside of the flanker. By this time, the quarterback knows the secondary is still in man-to-man coverage and that the safety is moving into a better position to cover the loop receiver. At this time, communication between the flanker, split end, and quarterback is very important. Our concern is not where the safety is playing, but where the corner is playing the split end. If the corner is playing the split end to the inside, the quarterback fakes a pass

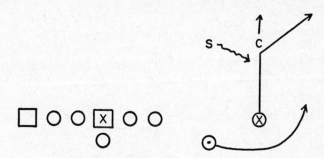

Figure 4.28 Split End Runs 2 Pattern Vs. Inside Corner Coverage.

Figure 4.29 Split End Runs 2-Go Pattern Vs. Outside Corner Coverage.

to the loop receiver and goes deep to the split end. If the corner is also moving over to stop the deep 2 pattern by the split end, a 2-go pattern is called (see Figures 4.28 and 4.29).

The terminology and strategies used in this offense allow you to attack any area of the field. Built-in reads and options give your receivers the edge they need to overcome any disadvantage they may face. The pro-T can be executed with a few simple plays or used to totally outgun the defense. For every defensive change that takes place during a game, you have the knowledge to put that change to use.

5

BLOCKING CONCEPTS IN THE PRO-T ATTACK

The pro-T blocking system has been designed for athletes who are not big enough to manhandle their opponents in a one-on-one situation. The blocking system relies more on intelligence than physical domination. Linemen are given an opportunity to select the type of block they feel is the most effective against their opponent. With a basic understanding of this flexible system, the average athlete has a chance to become an effective lineman.

HOLE NUMBERING SYSTEM

In the running game, all plays are called with two numbers. The first number represents the ball carrier and the second number identifies the main blocker. In the pro-T attack, the center is the 0 man. All linemen on the right are numbered 2, 4, 6, and 8, and on the left 1, 3, 5, and 7 (see Figure 5.1).

⑦   ⑤ ③ ① ⓪ ② ④ ⑥

⑧

Figure 5.1   Hole Numbering System.

Each position is given a number. This number represents the attack hole or point of attack. To show this, the play 32 dive is called. This means the number 3 back will be running through the number 2 holeman. Please note that this is not a gap type of numbering system. Later you will see why the backs run behind the hole man (see Figure 5.2). Unlike many offenses that provide each position with several blocking rules for every play, this offense uses a blocking call at the point of attack.

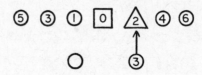

Figure 5.2   Attack Point Is the Number 2 Hole.

MAKING THE CALL

The snap cadence for the offense is ready, set, color, number, hut, hut, etc. Once the quarterback has called "ready," all members of the offensive line make a call. These calls consist of one or more words that inform other linemen how the play is to be blocked. The call made by the point-of-attack man applies to himself and the lineman on either side of him. All other calls made are only decoys. It is important to remember that all linemen must make a call on every play, even if the blocking pattern has already been predetermined. Figure 5.3 is an example of what takes place after *ready* has been called by the quarterback.

The number 4 man is the attack point and the call made by him only affects the number 2 and 6 blockers (see Figure 5.3).

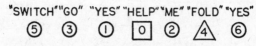

Figure 5.3   Lineman Making the Calls.

Base Call

The base call is used if the attack point blocker feels he is able to move the defender out of his hole in a man-to-man technique. If he feels this is the easiest block to use, he will call "base." In blocking base, this call applies to the man head up, on the holeman, over him and off the line of scrimmage, and the linebacker to his inside. To show the base call, the point of attack will be the number 2 hole. Below are three basic defenses in which the base call applies (see Figures 5.4, 5.5, and 5.6).

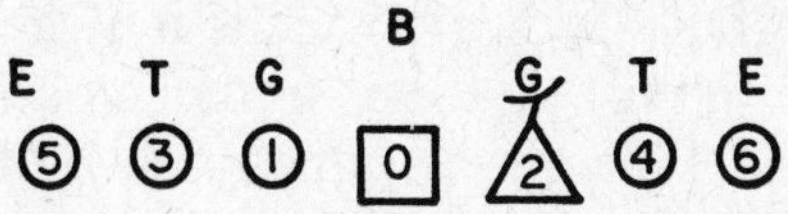

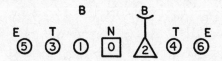

Figure 5.4   Base Call Vs. 6–1 (Man On).

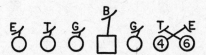

Figure 5.5   Base Call Vs. 5–2 (Man Over).

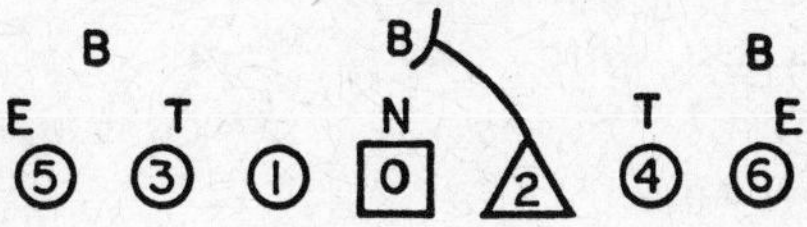

Figure 5.6   Base Call Vs. 5–3 (Linebacker to Inside).

The point-of-attack man is the only position that allows the blocker to vary from the base call. All other linemen follow the base-blocking rule. To illustrate this, the number 4 and 6 linemen are going to execute a cross block. Note that all other linemen are base blocking (see Figures 5.7 and 5.8).

Figure 5.7   Base Blocking Away from Attack Point.

Figure 5.8   Base Blocking Away from Attack Point.

Switch Me or You Call

The switch block is also referred to as the cross block. It is best noted for its angular blocking ability. The switch block is always performed with the point-of-attack lineman and his outside blocker. If the point of attack is at the number 3 hole, the number 5 lineman will be assisting in the switch block.

The live call is made by calling "switch." This lets the outside lineman know that he and the point man are going to perform the cross block. The second part of this call is the most important. When talking about the cross block, coaches feel that the outside man should always go first. In this offense the option is given to the holeman. As mentioned before, the call by the holeman is determined by the type of block he feels is easiest for him to make. In making the decision as to which blocker should go first, the holeman decides how tough the man in front of him is. If his man is extremely tough and strong, he may decide to have the tight end block down on his man and he will step around and block the defensive end. If this is his decision, the holeman calls "switch you." If the holeman's opponent is slow and not penetrating, he calls "switch me." In this case the holeman goes first, blocking the defensive end while the tight end blocks down on the defensive tackle. As an example, the number 4 holeman will be used to clarify this point (see Figures 5.9 and 5.10).

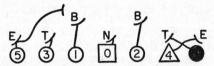

Figure 5.9 "Switch You" call by the number 4 holeman. The Tight End goes first. All other linemen base block.

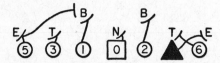

Figure 5.10 "Switch Me" call by the number 4 holeman. The Tight End goes second. All other linemen base block.

Fold Me or You Call

The fold block is similar to the cross block, except one of the defenders who is being blocked is off the line of scrimmage. In this situation the holeman has a critical decision to make. Since the linebacker is off the line, he has more range and mobility than a down lineman. The holeman has to decide whether to block the tackle or the roaming linebacker. With further game experience, the blockers will know which call will be most effective against the linebacker and defensive tackle.

The fold call is made exactly like the switch call. If the holeman feels that the linebacker is more critical to block, he calls "fold me." The holeman fires out and blocks the linebacker, and the tight end blocks down and picks up the defensive tackle (see Figure 5.11).

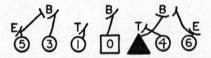

Figure 5.11 "Fold Me" call by the number 2 holeman. The holeman goes first. All other linemen base block.

If the tackle has been more effective against the run than the linebacker, the holeman calls "fold you." This tells the tight end that he goes first and blocks the defensive tackle. The holeman goes second and picks up the linebackers (see Figure 5.12). The number 2 man is chosen as the holeman.

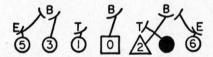

Figure 5.12 "Fold You" call by the number 2 holeman. The holeman goes second. All other linemen base block.

Help Call

The help call is used to pick up additional outside blocking to double team the defender at the point of attack. This call can be used at any time by the attack holeman. If the defense changes its alignment at the line of scrimmage, the help call becomes very useful. The help call also lets the ball carrier know he must run as tight as possible to the blocker's hip, directly outside the point of attack. With additional blocking support coming from the outside, the hole opens up quicker and moves to the outside. This is why the ball carrier must stay to the outside of the hole—and follow the hip of the outside blocker. To show an example of this, the 3 hole will be the attack point. The number 3 man calls "help." This lets the tight end know that he is to assist with the double team.

Figures 5.13 and 5.14 illustrate two blocking progressions. Diagram 5.13 shows the tight end's initial movement from the line. Diagram 5.14 demonstrates contact at the point of attack. The number 2 back runs off of the tight end's butt.

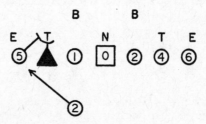

Figure 5.13   Start of the help block. Back follows butt of the number 5 holeman.

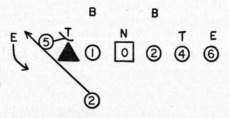

Figure 5.14   "Help" call by the number 3 blocker. Contact has been made by both the number 3 and number 5 blockers and the back follows the butt of the left tackle.

Yes Call

The yes call is simply a triple team block. This block involves the blockers to each side of the holeman and, again, can be called by the holeman at any time. This type of block is generally used in a short yardage situation or when the defense shifts into another defense and a large hole is open at the point of attack. Rather than waste time figuring out who to block, the yes call tells all three blockers to pour into the attack hole and block anyone in the way.

To illustrate this, the 32 dive is called. This is the right halfback through the number 2 man's attack point. The center, right guard, and right tackle block the left defensive tackle (see Figure 5.15).

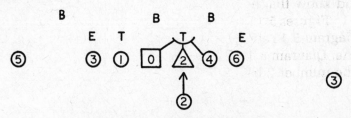

Figure 5.15   Yes Call—Triple Team.

The yes call is also used as an audible between the center and quarterback. If the center spots a linebacker moving in anticipation of the play, the center may call "yes." This lets the quarterback know that the quarterback sneak may be used. It is also the call for the triple team at the hole, 0.

Trap-Blocking Calls

Some pro-T formation blocks are called in the huddle rather than on the line of scrimmage. A typical block used in this example is the G-trap. The letter G identifies the offensive guard, and the word *trap* informs him that he will be pulling from the backside. In other words, if the play was going to the number 3 hole and the G-trap call was added to the play, the right guard would be trapping to his left (see Figure 5.16).

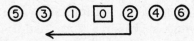

Figure 5.16   G-Trap—Offside Guard.

After the snap, the trap guard pulls to his left and starts his trap one holeman tighter than the attack point. This is done to prevent the guard from overrunning the defender being trapped. Also, if a linebacker blitzes and is missed by the playside blockers, the trapping guard could run into him unintentionally. This is not a normal practice, but it is another reason why the guard starts his trap one hole tighter. By colliding into the blitzing linebacker, the play may not be a success, but at least it may prevent a loss or fumble. As the guard pulls, all offensive linemen seal block away from the point of attack. To show a play in which the G-trap block is used, the play unbalanced right, 33, G-trap is called (see Figure 5.17).

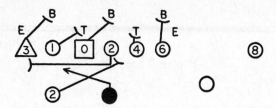

Figure   5.17   Right   Guard   Pulls   and   Blocks—G-Trap.

G-Block

As in the G-trap, the letter G identifies the guard as the key figure in the block. The word *block*, however, lets the playside guard know that he will trap. The playside guard will block a defensive end when the G-block is used.

The G-block is often difficult to execute because there are no two defensive ends who play the same. Some ends box, some crash, and some float along the line and read the blockers. These three techniques make it very difficult for the guard to make a clean block. We suggest the guard pull and run flat along the line of scrimmage. By making his pull flat, he will have time to adjust to all three types of defensive maneuvers. To show the G-block, the play pro-right, 24 blast, G-block is called. As in the G-trap, all offensive linemen not involved in the G-block seal away from the G-block (see Figure 5.18).

Both the G-trap and G-block are used to give additional blocking support when a play cannot be blocked with calls made by the point of attack. There are specific plays in which the G-trap and G-block are used, but in certain game situations the blocking scheme may have to be changed and the guards will be called on for additional blocking. To show how one

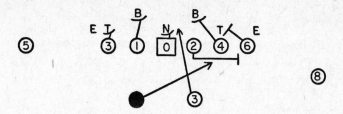

Figure 5.18   G-Blocking by Right Guard.

specific play can be blocked with several variations, the play 24 blast is used. The 24 blast is the basic off-tackle play which involves a halfback (blast) lead block. Figures 5.19, 5.20, and 5.21 show several ways in which this play can be blocked.

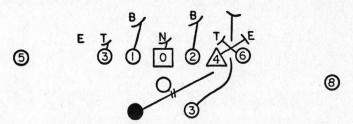

Figure 5.19   24 Blast "Switch Me" Call by the Number 4 Holeman.

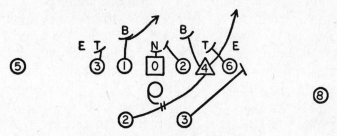

Figure 5.20   24 Blast, H-Block.

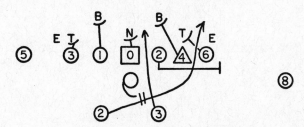

Figure 5.21   24 Blast, G-Block.

Power Block

The word *power* informs both guards that they will pull in the same direction. The power block is a combination of both the G-block and G-trap. The playside guard pulls, leads the play, and the offside guard traps the hole left vacant by the playside guard. An example of this play is the 28 power sweep. As in all pulling and trapping plays, members of the offensive line seal block away from the point of attack (see Figure 5.22).

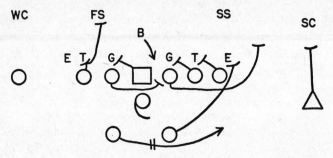

Figure 5.22   Pro Right, 28 Power Sweep.

Seal Blocking

There are certain plays in the running attack that require seal blocking. The letters G or H (see halfback blocking) have no significance to other members of the line. The word *trap* or *block*, however, lets all blockers on the line know that they are to seal block. In seal blocking, each offensive lineman blocks one man down, either on or off of the line of scrimmage, away from the play. Seal blocking can be more easily performed against six-, seven-, and eight-man lines than those defenses that employ three or four linebackers. The linebackers are more mobile because of their position off the line. The seal block is a cutoff block, not to be confused with the cut down or chop block.

When performing the seal block, the offensive lineman is taught to make contact in the body region of the defender between the waist and shoulder pads. He is trying to stand the defender up and limit his view of the ball carrier. In the pro-T attack the seal block should never be thrown below the waist. First, a low block will take the offensive lineman out of the play, limiting their downfield blocking ability. Second, and most important, because of the angle blocking involved, a low block could be harmful to the knee area of the high school athlete. When executing the seal block, the lineman makes inside shoulder contact with the inside shoulder of the defender. When referring to inside, we are talking about the relationship of the blocker to the play. To show you an example of seal blocking the play 28 power sweep is used (see Figure 5.23).

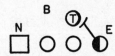

Figure 5.23   Seal Blocking Technique.

Downfield Blocking

One of the most important phases of the ground attack is the support given downfield by the offensive line. In many cases, this can make or break the big play. Downfield blocking rules have been simplified in the pro-T attack. These rules cover all running plays with the exception of the plays in which seal blocking is used, as in the case of the G-trap, G-block, and H-block. One very important item that should be emphasized to your athletes is that they should always make contact with a defender on the line of scrimmage or off the line as in the case of a linebacker, before releasing downfield into the secondary. There are two rules to be followed when downfield blocking.

Rule 1: 2-hole rule

If the ball is run anywhere between the 6 hole on the right and the 5 hole on the left, all blockers positioned further out than two complete holes outside the point of attack are to go downfield and block the closest defensive back to the original point of attack.

By referring to two complete holemen, we are referring to two blockers on either side of the point of attack. To show an example of this, the 1 hole is used as the attack point. The 5, 3, 0, and 2 holemen are within the 2-hole rule, therefore they will block the area of the running play. The 7, 4, and 6 offensive blockers are located outside of the blocking zone, so they will go downfield and block the defensive backs (see Figure 5.24).

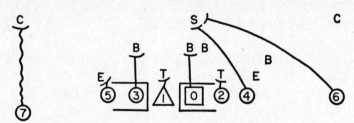

Figure 5.24   Rule 1: Downfield Blocking—2 Hole Rule.

Rule 2: 3-hole rule

If the ball is run in the area of the 7 and 8 holes, the 2-hole rule is replaced with the 3-hole rule. Those blockers who are within three holemen to the inside of the attack point holeman block the play accordingly. The outside receiver always blocks base, since he is always in the man-to-man blocking situation. To illustrate this, the play 28 power sweep is used. The number 8 man is the point-of-attack man and blocks base. The number 2, 4, and 6 men are within the 3-hole rule and block the play accordingly. The 0 man, 1, 3, and 5 blockers make contact with the closest defender and head downfield on the safety positions. The number 5 blocker is again in the base blocking situation (see Figure 5.25).

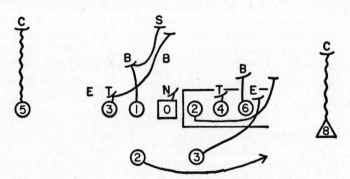

Figure 5.25   Rule 2: Downfield Blocking— 3-Hole Rule.

Downfield Blocking in the Trapping Game

The G-trap blocking system has trap plays from the 5 hole on the left to the 6 hole on the right. Since seal blocking is used in the G-trap blocking scheme, all linemen on the side of the line where the G-trap is taking place are to use seal blocking.

Those linemen to the backside of the G-trap guard base block, and then head downfield. The 5 and 8 blockers who are the wide receivers base block also as they are heading downfield. To illustrate this point, the play 31 G-trap is used against the 52 defense (see Figure 5.26).

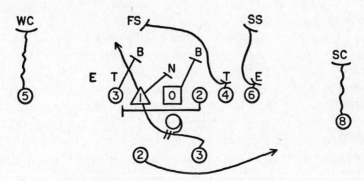

Figure 5.26 Downfield Blocking for G-Trap Blocking.

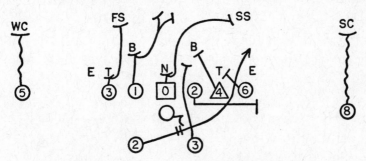

Figure 5.27 Downfield Blocking for G-Blocking.

You will notice that the number 3, 1, and 0 holemen are seal blocking. The number 2 lineman, the backside guard, is G-trapping. The number 4 and 6 men are base blocking and then heading downfield to pick up their respective opponents.

The G-block is always used to block the outside holes such as the 5, 6, and 7. When the G-block is called to the 5 or 6 hole, all linemen seal block on the side of the play. Those linemen on the backside of the G-block again base block and go downfield. The outside receivers base block (see Figure 5.27).

Downfield Blocking in the Power Call

Remember the power call involves both the G-trap and G-block. The playside guard leads the point of attack and the G-trap guard fills the hole left by the pulling G-blocker. In plays where the power call is added, all offensive blockers, including the outside receiver, seal block. The blockers on the backside of the G-trap guard base block their opponent and release downfield. The backside receiver also base blocks. In seal blocking, the outside receiver on the playside picks up the first defender off the line to his side. This may be an outside linebacker or playside safety. To show this, the play 37 power sweep is used (see Figure 5.28).

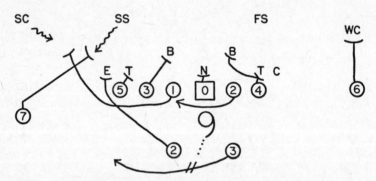

Figure 5.28   Downfield Block for the Power Call.

Drop-Back Pass Protection

In the pro-T attack, drop-back passing without the use of play action is used very sparingly. The drop-back pass limits the quarterback's running ability and gives the defense a better chance to contain the passer. You may want to integrate part of this attack into your basic offense for slowfooted quarterbacks. For this reason, drop-back protection is given.

The drop-back protection is based on a combination of man-to-man and zone or area blocking. Each line position has basic rules that apply to all defenses. These rules are as follows:

Center: Block 0 hole only. The offensive center acts as a pivot point in line blocking. He never helps another blocker or moves out of the 0 hole.

Guards: Block man on; slide to inside gap. The guards block any defender on or off the line of scrimmage in a man-to-man technique (pushing him to the out-side). If there is a linebacker on the guard but off the line of scrimmage and not blitzing, the guard slides to the inside gap and double teams with the center.

Tackles: Block man on; slide to outside gap. This rule is the same as the guards' if there is a man on the tackle or a linebacker off the line. If there is no defender on or off the line of scrimmage, the tackle slides to the gap outside of his position. In this case, the tackle may pick up an outside blitzing linebacker or defensive end.

In drop-back protection, influence blocking is used. The offensive lineman steps forward with his inside foot and pivots off his outside heel. By doing this, the offensive lineman opens up an outside alley for the pass rusher. As the defender penetrates into that alley, the offensive lineman always pushes him to the outside. Contact by the lineman must be continuous in order to ride the defenders outside. Figures 5.29, 5.30, 5.31, and 5.32 are examples of how the drop-back pass blocking rules are applied to various defenses.

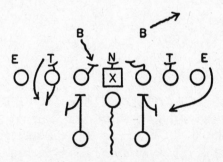

Figure 5.29   Rule Blocking Vs. 5–2.

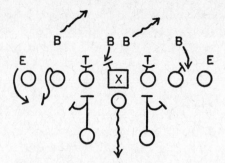

Figure 5.30   Rule Blocking Vs. 4–4.

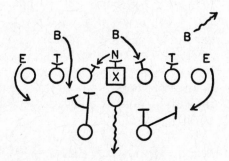

Figure 5.31   Rule Blocking Vs. 5–3.

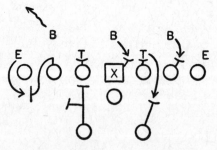

Figure 5.32   Rule Blocking Vs. 4–3.

Quick Pass Protection

This type of protection is used when the pop, fire, and shoot passing patterns are called.

The quick patterns take about 1 or 2 seconds to complete, so a quick type of block is used. Linemen who have defenders directly in front of them and on the line must fire out and make aggressive contact. In making contact, the linemen attempt to put either shoulder into the waist of the defender. By doing this, it forces the defensive lineman to stay low and prevents them from tipping the pass as it is thrown. Offensive linemen who have linebackers on them fire out in a low position as if they were going to block the defenders. In firing out they only take two steps. This should put them one step past the line of scrimmage at which time the linebacker should have stepped up to make contact. Again, their block should be about waist high. If the linebacker steps up into the block, he has taken himself out of the play (see Figure 5.33).

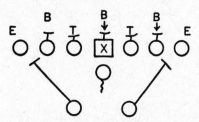

Figure 5.33   Quick Pass Protection.

Roll-Out Protection

Roll-out, like drop-back protection uses influence blocking. The blocking rules are very similar to those used in drop-back protection, except one additional movement is required. The rules for roll-out protection are as follows:

Center:	Block 0 hole, backside. The center remains in the 0 hole. If a defender penetrates to his backside, he picks him up.
Guards and tackles:	Man on, blitzing backer, backside. As in the drop-back pass protection, the guards and tackles block the man on the line of scrimmage first. If no defender is on the line, the guards and tackles pick up the blitzing linebacker. If no linebackers are blitzing, they block the gap to their backside.

To show how these rules apply, Figures 5.34, 5.35, 5.36, and

5.37 illustrate these blocking rules against several different types of defenses.

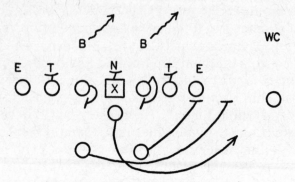

Figure 5.34   Roll Right Protection Vs. 5–2.

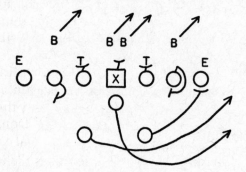

Figure 5.35   Roll Right Protection Vs. 4–4 or Split 6.

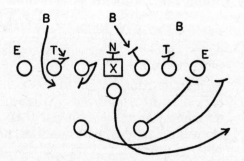

Figure 5.36   Roll Right Protection Vs. 5–3.

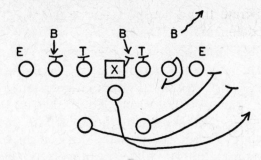

Figure 5.37   Roll Right Protection Vs. 4–3.

Play-Action Protection

Play-action protection uses both the drop-back and roll-out techniques. The play-action side of the formation instructs the offensive lineman to fire out at all defenders on or off the line of scrimmage. Once contact is made, offensive linemen to the action side retreat into their normal positions and begin following the drop-back protection rules.

The weak side or side not involved with the play action, fires out as in quick pass protection. Once contact is made, they retreat into their normal positions and follow the roll-out blocking rules as if the ball was being run away from them. In other words, they block the backside for a normal roll-out pass. To show an example of this the play pro left, 24 blast action, 25, X-go is used (see Figure 5.38).

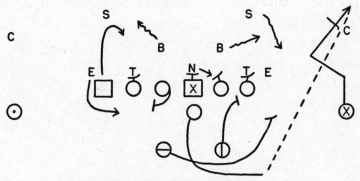

Figure 5.38   Play Action Protection Vs. 5–2

The blocking concept of the pro-T offense has been specifically designed to aid athletes who do not have outstanding ability. Built-in options give each player choices that enable him to make decisions concerning his particular block. To eliminate confusion, a two-rule blocking system has been set up to simplify downfield blocking. The athlete no longer has to memorize specific blocking assignments. The pass blocking phase of the pro-T is not complicated but still provides several types of pass protection and gives the offense more flexibility in its attack.

6

COACHING THE PRO-T BACKFIELD

This chapter discusses the entire backfield phase of the pro-T offense. An explanation of how the backs read holes, backfield pass patterns, and the back's role in pass protection blocking is included.

RUNNING TO DAYLIGHT

The concept of the running game need no rely on the super-talented athlete or the big fullback-type players. It should rely on the ability of the running backs to follow effective keys. Because of the nature of the pro-T blocking system the backs no longer have to be fast and big to be successful.

Chapter 5 deals with offensive line blocking. You will note that the linemen screen block the defenders rather than blow them out of the hole. For this reason, the backs are taught to run behind the butt of the point of attack man. By running to the lineman's butt, the back always has the blocker between him and the defensive player. This basic rule helps the backs in two ways:

1. The backs have a specific point that they follow in order to hit the correct hole. By watching the holeman, they can explode quickly to the designated area.

2. By following the attack man, the backs don't have to rely on natural ability to read the blocks by the offensive line in order to find daylight.

When using this system, you may find that if your players follow the holeman's butt, the hole may open between two defenders, one holeman to either side of the designated hole, or completely outside of the designed hole, as in a trap block.

Diagrams 6.1 and 6.2 illustrate the running back following the holeman's butt. The illustrations are shown as though the offensive blockers had already performed their blocks. Each blocker is listed by his hole number.

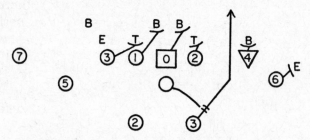

Figure 6.1   34 dive. The right halfback follows the number 4 man's butt (base blocking call).

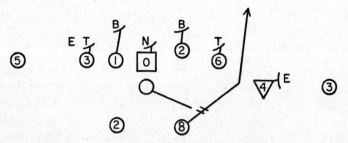

Figure 6.2   34 dive. The right halfback follows the number 4 man's butt ("switch you" call).

As the figure shows, the back follows the block of the holeman's butt. Also, you can see that both holes vary where the ball carrier is running.

As in all running plays, the ball carrier must run to where the attack holeman was originally positioned before he breaks and follows the butt of the holeman. This makes the blocking easier for the offensive lineman, since the defensive pursuit follows the back's initial movement and reacts to it. It also makes it easier for the quarterback to make a consistent handoff if he knows where the backs are going.

HALFBACK PATTERNS

Because of the wide variety of formations used in the pro-T offense, the running backs must know all the patterns being used in the total passing attack. Besides these, there are two specific patterns that the backs must be able to perform: the loop pattern, covered in chapter 4, and the flare pattern. The loop pattern is primarily used to isolate a back on a linebacker or defensive end. This pattern is often used against defenses that do a lot of blitzing from the outside linebacker positions or have two linebackers inside, such as 5–2 or 6–2 defenses.

By looping the backs, two things take place.

1. If a linebacker is blitzing, the loop receiver will be uncovered in the flats area.
2. If the linebacker leaves his area to pick up the loop receiver, his zone will be open for a curl or quick slant pattern by the wide receiver or tight end.

When running the loop pattern, the back runs parallel along the line of scrimmage until he is outside the coverage of the outside linebacker or defensive end. Once outside, he breaks his pattern upfield at a 45 degree angle. To show an illustration of this, the right halfback is used. The play is called slot right, 256, R-loop (see Figure 6.3).

This particular pattern is a play that requires the quarterback and receiver to read the defense. It can be used effectively against any type of defense. When using this pattern, the offense concentrates on the flats and short curl areas to the loop side. Both the quarterback and loop receiver key the outside

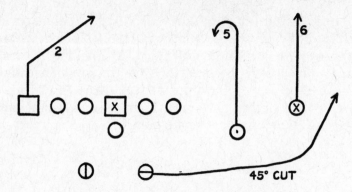

Figure 6.3   R-Loop Pattern by Right Halfback.

linebacker. If the linebacker follows the loop receiver, the running back continues to run his pattern parallel along the line of scrimmage until he is far enough outside the linebacker to turn upfield. By doing this, the loop receiver clears out the curl area by pulling the linebacker into a man-to-man coverage. The quarterback has read that the linebacker is gone and the curl zone is open for the 5 pattern by the flanker (see Figure 6.4).

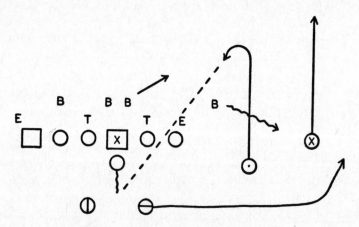

Figure 6.4   Quarterback Read Vs. Linebacker Coverage on Loop Receiver.

If the outside linebacker senses the flanker curling behind him, he may not follow the loop receiver. If both the loop receiver and quarterback see this, the right halfback turns upfield earlier and the quarterback passes to him.

At times, you may want to isolate the loop receiver on the outside linebacker or defensive end. To do this, a pick pattern may have to be used. In order to prevent the linebacker from picking up the back, he must be screened out so that he cannot cover the looping receiver. Screening out refers to a pattern or movement that can be used to distract or decoy the linebackers from picking up the back quickly. When the pick is used, the outside receiver runs a pattern across the face of the linebacker, or curls just to the outside of the linebacker's position. The slot man runs a deep corner pattern to divert the defensive back from supporting the flats area. When this action is used, the loop receiver must get to the flats quickly, as the linebacker is tied up inside (see Figure 6.5).

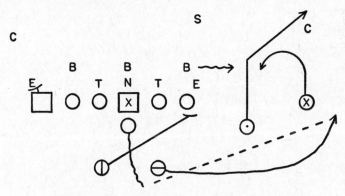

Figure 6.5   Pick Pattern Used to Isolate Loop Receiver.

FLARE PATTERN

The flare pattern is similar to the loop pattern in that it is basically used against linebackers. When the flare pattern is performed, roll-out or play-action passing is used.

The flare pattern can be executed to either the strong or weak side, although certain situations dictate which back is to be used. When the flare pattern is called, the back not involved in the pattern always attacks the playside defensive end. This applies to both roll-out and play-action protection. Certain defensive philosophies require the defensive ends to crash on every play. Others specify that defensive ends box or float along the line of scrimmage and string the play out.

When facing the crashing end, it is wise to flare the backside halfback and use the playside halfback to pick up the crashing end. By stopping the crashing end early, the quarterback has time to get out of the pocket. To illustrate this play, the call pro left, roll right, 236, L-flare is used. The left halfback runs between the crashing defensive end and the left defensive tackle (see Figure 6.6).

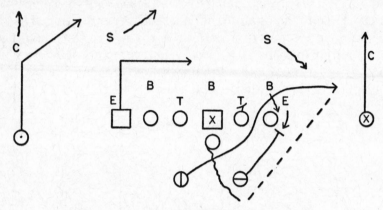

Figure 6.6   L-Flare Vs. Crashing Linebacker.

As the left halfback is entering the crease between the defensive end and tackle, he makes a read on the linebacker. If the linebacker has not taken the play-action fake and dropped back into his zone, the flare halfback cuts his pattern short and breaks quickly into the flats. This widens the distance between the linebacker and flare halfback. If the linebacker comes up to support the roll-out quarterback, the flare receiver runs his pattern deep to gain more yardage (see Figures 6.7 and 6.8).

When using the flare pattern, one receiver should take the safety deep and out of the flare receiver's area. If the corner supports the flats and the safety moves over to take the split end in a man-to-man coverage, the deep post pattern will be open.

When facing the boxing defensive end, there are two areas that should be looked at. First, the end who strings the play out by boxing or floating along the line of scrimmage normally has an outside responsibility on all plays. This means that inside run support comes from the playside linebacker. Because of this, the quarterback expects the playside linebacker to come

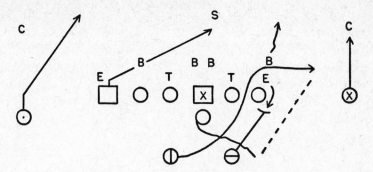

Figure 6.7 Flare Vs. Linebacker Drop.

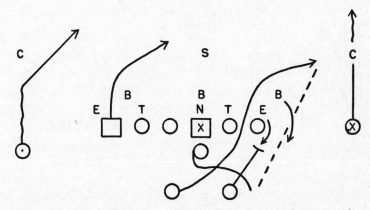

Figure 6.8 Flare Vs. Linebacker Support.

up hard between the boxing defensive end and the defensive tackle. To control this, the quarterback flares the playside back into the flats area early. The halfback explodes off tackle and runs his pattern approximately 10 yards downfield before breaking to the sideline. The offside halfback concentrates on picking up the playside linebacker. The left halfback's angle starts at the off-tackle hole and flattens out as he sees the linebacker move in. The back must make sure that he drives the linebacker to the outside (see Figure 6.9).

Another defensive variation is the boxing end and the floating linebacker combination. This creates more of a problem because the flare back is now required to make a read on the floating linebacker rather than the floating end. In this situation a roll-out pass moves the linebackers so the flare back can make

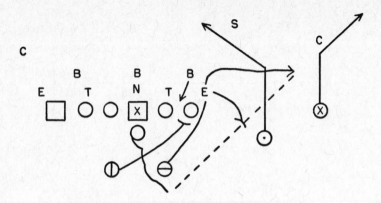

Figure 6.9   Flare Vs. Floating End and Crashing Linebacker.

the read. If a drop-back or play-action pass is used, the linebacker is not fooled since he is already protecting the flats area.
When roll-out action is used, the quarterback has two choices.
He can sprint to the sidelines and pull the linebacker with him,
or he can roll out short and hold the linebacker in place. The
quarterback's action is determined by the defensive end's
movement and the blocking ability of the blocking back (see
Figures 6.10 and 6.11).

In Figure 6.10, the short roll-out action has held the linebacker's movement to the outside. The flare back reads this and
runs his pattern deeper and cuts to the sideline.

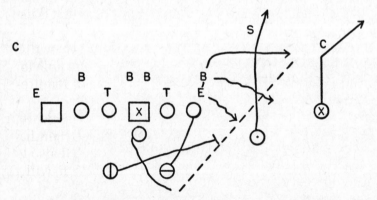

Figure 6.10   Short Roll-Out Action Used to
Hold the Linebacker in Position.

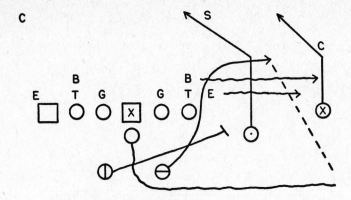

Figure 6.11 Long Roll-Out Action Used to Move the Linebacker Out of Position.

The flare back in Figure 6.11 watches the linebacker move with the quarterback. The back slows his pattern and remains behind the linebacker's coverage. This pattern may require the flare back to come to a complete stop rather than continue his pattern to the sideline. The flare back must make sure he has found an open seam in the linebacker's coverage.

BACKFIELD BLOCKING

In the pro-T attack, the blocking scheme used by the backfield is limited to three calls. Two of these calls are incorporated into the play and the third is a predetermined block that is used with pulling guards.

The blast call informs the playside halfback that he will fill the hole the ball carrier is running through or fill the hole for a guard who is pulling. In other words, the word *blast* requires a halfback lead somewhere in the offensive line.

To illustrate this, an off-tackle play is used. The quarterback calls the play pro-right, 24, blast. This lets the right halfback know he will lead the play through the 4 hole. It also lets the linemen know that additional blocking strength will be given from the backfield (see Figure 6.12).

In this offense, there are certain plays that require the blast block but do not use the word *blast* in the play call. Two of these

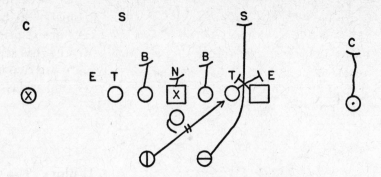

Figure 6.12   Blast Lead by Right Halfback.

plays are the G-trap and G-block. The G-trap and G-block are
calls to let the guards know they will trap or pull. These calls
also let the backs know they must fill the hole left when the

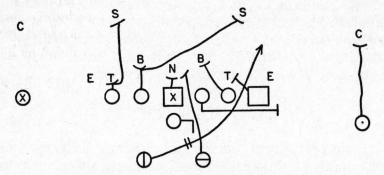

Figure 6.13   24 Blast, G-Block. Right Halfback
Fills Hole Left by Pulling Guard.

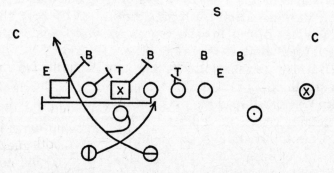

Figure 6.14   Cross Buck, G-Trap. Left Halfback Fills Hole Left by Trapping Guard.

guards are used for additional blocking. The blast block is used to fill these holes, and in this case, the backs are required to block a defender in holes where the guards were. This seals off any further penetration by the defenders. Here are two examples of using the blast block where both the G-trap and G-block calls are used (see Figures 6.13 and 6.14).

H-Block

A variation of the blast block is the H-block. The major difference is, rather than filling a hole left by the guards or leading a hole that has already been opened up by the line, the halfback is solely responsible for blocking the hole. When the H-block is called, the line knows they seal block away from the play, and the playside back kicks out the defender in the hole. The H-block can be used for any running play and is an effective tool when additional blocking is needed. To show an example of the H-block, the play 33, H-block is called. The left halfback attacks the 3 hole and kicks out any defender he sees (see Figure 6.15).

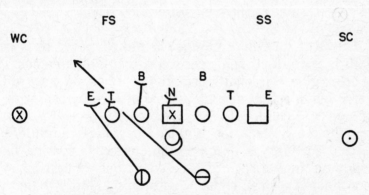

Figure 6.15   H-Block Kick Out by the Left Halfback.

When an H-block adjustment is needed, the quarterback may add it to any running play with the exception of the power sweep. When the power sweep is executed, both guards pull to the power side. To help these guards turn the corner, the H-block is required from the playside back. The H-block back must attack the defensive end from the inside out position. He has to maintain the correct blocking angle on the defensive end in case the end is crashing. On the other hand, if the defensive end is boxing or stringing the play out, the back must stay with his block and ride the end outside so the guards may turn upfield early (see Figure 6.16).

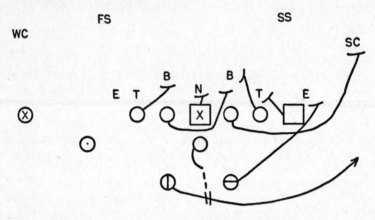

Figure 6.16   H-Block for Power Sweep Action.

BACKFIELD PASS PROTECTION

The least deceptive play is the straight drop-back pass with little or no faking being performed by the quarterback. The drop back gives the quarterback the best overall view of the patterns being run. It also gives the defense the best view of the play.

In the pro-T attack, the drop-back pass in its purest form is seldom used. First, it limits the quarterback's passing time. Second, the quarterback is isolated in one central location where the defense can contain his running ability. When the drop-back pass is used, both backs attack the line as if they are receiving a handoff. As the quarterback fakes and starts his retreat, both backs retreat into a two-point stance approximately three yards from the line of scrimmage. They key the center guard gap and watch for onrushing linemen. Once they are certain that the offensive linemen have picked up any rush, they focus their attention on the gap between the guard and offensive tackle. If a defender has penetrated, the backs pick them up by attacking them in the upper body, forcing them to the outside. This allows the quarterback to step up into the pocket if more time is needed to get the pass off (see Figure 6.17).

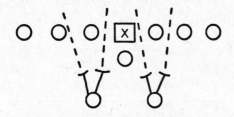

Figure 6.17   Drop-Back Protection.

When flare and loop patterns are run with drop-back passing, some defenses may force the tight end to stay and block the backside. In this case, the backside halfback picks up the playside defensive end. A typical play is the pro left, drop back, 20X, R-loop (see Figure 6.18).

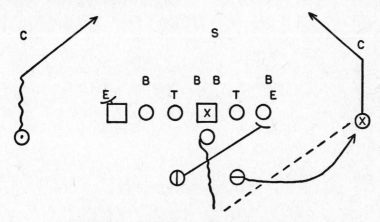

Figure 6.18   Tight End Used for Drop-Back Protection.

ROLL-OUT PROTECTION

When using roll-out protection the quarterback attempts to get outside the containment as quickly as possible. Then the roll-side back must attack the defensive end, whether he is crashing or boxing. The offense cannot allow the quarterback to be contained. As the playside halfback performs his H-block on the defensive end, he attempts to either knock the defender off his feet, or make contact and drive the defenders backward. The H-block back must maintain control and not let the defensive end move to his outside.

The backside halfback explodes to the roll side at a 30 degree angle. He keys the defensive end and picks him up if the roll-side back has missed his block. If the defensive end has been sufficiently picked up by the H-block back, the backside halfback continues to run parallel along the line of scrimmage and picks up any additional defenders (see Figure 6.19).

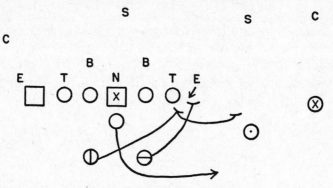

Figure 6.19   Roll Right Protection.

The roll-out pass is referred to as roll right or roll left. This lets the backs know who is H-blocking and who is lead blocking for the quarterback.

QUICK PROTECTION

This type of protection is used when a receiver is isolated in one specific pattern. A pattern of this type is the fire, shoot, and pop. These patterns require only one to two seconds of pass protection. Because of this, both backs aggressively attack the defensive ends on their side. This is done to keep the defensive end from tipping the pass. This also assists the quarterback in case the quarterback sees a play open up but doesn't have time to change the play. He still has time to drop back and set up if he has to throw deep. In quick protection, the backs take an inside out angle when firing out at the defenders.

Quick protection is not called in the huddle. Anytime pop, fire, and shoot patterns are called as isolation patterns, quick protection is used by the backs (see Figure 6.20).

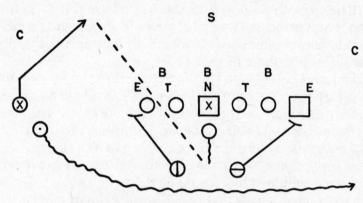

Figure 6.20 Twins Left, Z-Even, X-Pop (Quick Protection).

PLAY-ACTION PROTECTION

Play-action protection is the type most widely used in the pro-T attack. Play action does several things.

1. It gives the defensive line the impression that the ball is being run. Their initial charge is then directed at the action rather than at the quarterback.
2. It allows the offense to control linebackers' movement. By faking the run, the linebackers are forced to support the run before dropping into their normal defensive passing zones.
3. It forces the secondary into making a commitment. By watching how the secondary adjusts to various movements, the offense can set up future plays.

The pro-T attack uses play action from every formation. The type of pass thrown dictates the type and amount of protection needed. In the play-action series, the short pass, as well as the deep pass, can be executed with equal effectiveness.

When play-action passing is used, both sides of the formation must be covered. This may require the tight end to stay in and block, or the flanker to come in motion and pick up the blind side pass rush. The entire play-action protection series is coordinated with motion and the use of the 0 pass pattern, which requires the designated receiver to stay in and block. To illustrate the combination involved in setting up the play-action blocking, three examples are given.

The least complicated of the three is the cross-buck action. This action involves only the backs. No additional blocking is needed by the tight end or flanker. When the cross-buck action is used, one back takes off just ahead of the other. To identify the action being used, the quarterback calls it as if the normal cross buck is being executed. In this play, the ball carrier and hole are given. An example of this would be the 24 cross buck. The call tells the number 2 back that he will run to the number 4 hole. Since the 2 back is the primary ball carrier, he waits until the number 3 back has cleared in front of him before he begins his approach to the line. In deciding which cross-buck action to use, the quarterback should make sure that his blind side is being protected first. An example of this would be the pro right, 24 cross-buck action, X3X (see Figure 6.21).

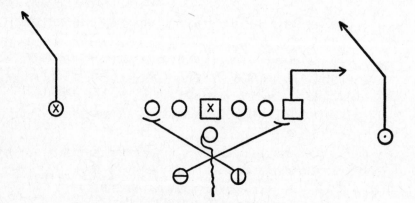

Figure 6.21   Right Halfback Goes First and Blocks the Blind Side.

Another type of action used is the off-tackle blast. Because both ball carriers attack one side of the formation, the tight end may have to block the backside.

The 0 pattern requires the designated receiver to stay in and block rather than become involved in the pass pattern. If additional blocking is needed on the backside, the quarterback gives the tight end the 0 pattern. This type of blocking is needed when the flare and loop patterns are used or when the offense is in the trips formation. An example of this is the play slot right, 24 blast action, 0, X, 2, R-flare (see Figure 6.22).

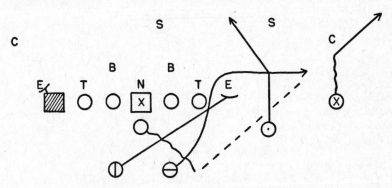

Figure 6.22   Play Action Blast with Tight End Blocking.

The last type of action used in the pro-T attack uses the flanker as an additional blocker. Again, we use the 0 pattern to let the flanker know that he will pick up the backside pressure.

As the flanker is used in blocking, he may be motioned in front of the running backs as in the counteraction, or behind the backs to simulate his normal pattern. Either movement by the flanker gives him the element of surprise as he picks up the defensive end.

To illustrate a typical play in which the flanker is used to block the backside, we call the pro left, Z-even, 33 dive action, 0X9, L-loop (see Figure 6.23).

The 0 pattern called in this play informs the flanker that he will pick up the pass rush on the even side of the formation.

In all three types of action, the blockers, either backs, tight end, or flanker can be used as a delay receiver. An example of

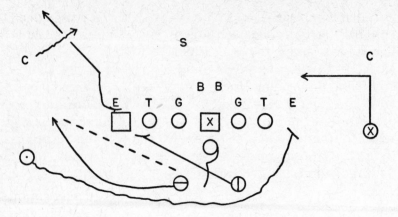

Figure 6.23   Motion Used for Pass Protection.

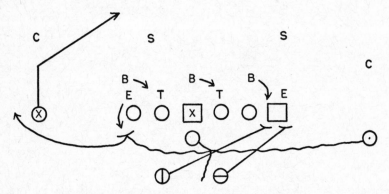

Figure 6.24   Flanker Blocking with the Addition of the Delay Loop Pattern.

this type of play is the call, pro right, Z-odd, 24 blast action, 2, 0, Z-delay loop (see Figure 6.24).

The Z-odd call informs the motion man that he will block the defensive pass rusher to the odd side. With the addition of the Z-delay loop call, the motion man hits the pass rusher, stays with him for one complete second, then releases his blocker and executes the loop pattern. With the 24 blast action incorporated into this type of play, the linebackers should move in the direction to the side of the action. With the split end running a 2 pattern, the defensive corner should clear deep and out of position to cover the motion man as he continues his loop pattern. As the weak side defensive end makes contact with the motion man, he takes himself out of position and enables him from covering the loop receiver.

SINGLE BACK BLOCKING

In the pro-T offense, there are several formations using only one back in the backfield. You, as the offensive coach, may see several defensive formations attempting to stop the plays developing from these formations. If a basic three- or four-man rush is used to contain the offense, your normal play-action and drop-back protection by the offensive line will be adequate

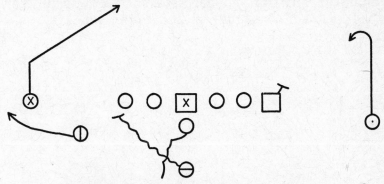

Figure 6.25   Single Back Blocking with Tight End Help.

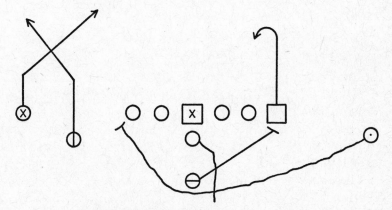

Figure 6.26   Single Back Blocking with Help for the Flankers.

enough to protect the quarterback. In this situation, the solo halfback always blocks to the side of the formation that is on the blind side of the quarterback as he drops back. The tight end and flanker can also be used if the defense begins to use stunts with their linebackers or defensive linemen.

When additional blocking by the tight end and flanker is used, the solo back blocks to the opposite side of their block. Figures 6.25 and 6.26 illustrate solo back blocking with the addition of outside help.

This chapter has given you the basics you need to coach the pro-T backfield. All areas of backfield play have been explained and diagrammed. From reading and understanding the terminologies used and concepts behind these formations, you, as the backfield coach, will be able to put your phase of the attack together.

7

GAINING CONFIDENCE WITH
THE INSIDE GAME

Chapter 7 covers the basics of the inside ground game. The dive and cross-buck series are explained as vital running plays, as well as deceptive play-action strategy for the passing attack.

THE DIVE SERIES

The least complicated of all running plays is the dive. This play can be directed into any hole, although it is most effective when kept within the boundaries of the tackles. There are four basic dive plays used in this attack.

When diving behind the offensive guards, the quarterback uses a reverse pivot. This action is used to manipulate the defense into reacting in the direction away from the play. The back opposite the ball carrier loops to the direction away from the dive.

When using the dive through the 3 and 4 holes, a straight line handoff is used. The quarterback runs parallel along the line of scrimmage and hands off to the designated back. The back opposite the ball carrier runs parallel along the line to the same side as the play. This is simply a veer action with the handoff to the lead back (see Figures 7.1, 7.2, 7.3, and 7.4).

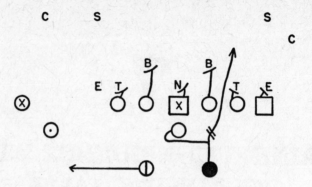

Figure 7.1   Twins Left, 32 Dive (Base Blocking).

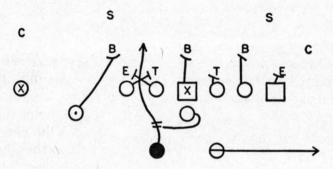

Figure 7.2   Slot Left, 21 Dive (Switch Blocking).

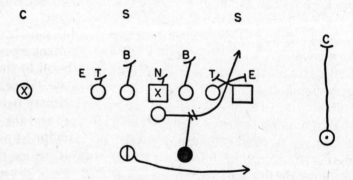

Figure 7.3   Pro Right, 34 Dive (Switch Blocking).

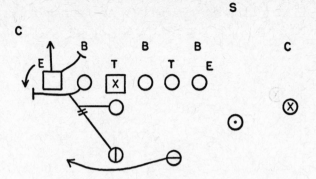

Figure 7.4   Unbalanced Right, 23 Dive (Fold Blocking).

DELAY DIVE (DRAW) SERIES

With the use of quick pattern passing fakes and motion from the backfield, the dive play can become one of the most effective plays in your arsenal.

The quick pass fake by the quarterback helps this play in two ways. First, by using this fake it stops the charge of the defensive line and gives the offensive blockers the advantage of momentum as they are firing out of their stance. Second, the defense reacts by dropping back, allowing the back to hit the hole before the defense can adjust and move to the ball. Although these plays are classified as dive plays, they may also be used as a quick draw or delay draw.

When executing the dives from the quick pass action, the quarterback takes one step back, plants, and fakes a pass to the quick receiver. He reverse pivots and hands off to the designated ball carrier. As this action is taking place, the other back loops to the side of the quick pattern. The primary ball carrier stays in his stance, with one hand on the ground for 1½ seconds. When he sees that the quarterback has made the pass fake, he explodes to the designated hole. For simplification this play has been labeled as a delay draw (see Figures 7.5, 7.6, and 7.7).

The pass-action dives can also be executed by faking a pass to a back in motion. A linebacker often pulls out of his normal position to cover the motion back. With the use of the slot, a back in motion to the slot side draws additional attention from the linebacker.

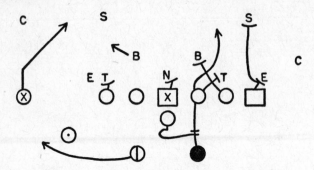

Figure 7.5   Slot Left, X-Pop Action, 32 Delay Draw.

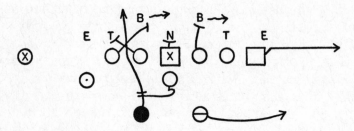

Figure 7.6   Tight Slot Left, Y-Fire Action, 21 Delay Draw.

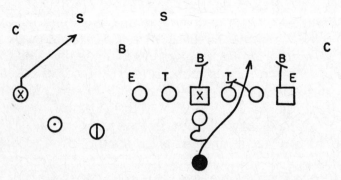

Figure 7.7   Trips Left, X-Pop Action, 32 Delay Draw.

OPTIONAL DIVE PLAYS FOR PASS ACTION

In this case, the quarterback takes one step back and fakes a pass to the motion man. Then he takes one additional step towards the designated hole and hands off to the primary ball carrier. The ball carrier does not wait one full second before taking off. As the ball is snapped, he pauses momentarily before hitting the hole. This gives the quarterback time to fake the pass and take his additional step (see Figures 7.8 and 7.9).

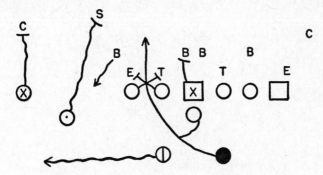

Figure 7.8   Slot Left, L-Odd Action, 33 Dive.

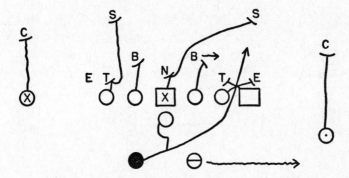

Figure 7.9   Pro Right, R-Even Action, 24 Dive.

Many other play-action fakes can be used to disguise this fundamental play. Motion is often used to move linebackers out of position either by moving them out to cover motion or getting them to relax as the motion is moving away from them.

One of the most effective dive plays in this attack is the dive to the motion side with a quick-pitch action to the playside back. As motion comes to the playside, the outside linebacker cheats out to maintain outside control. With the quick-pitch action fake to the playside, many defensive ends are drawn to the outside. With these two defenders moving to the outside, there is a crease between the defensive tackle and defensive end (see Figure 7.10).

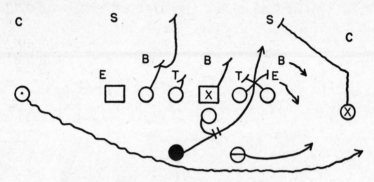

Figure 7.10   Pro Left, Z-Even, 38 Quick Pitch, 24 Dive.

In this play, the quarterback reverse pivots and fakes the quick-pitch action to the right halfback. As he fakes this action, he holds the ball waist-high and hands off to the trailing halfback who explodes to the hole on the snap.

In goal line situations, the defensive end may be easily influenced towards the outside with the use of motion or the

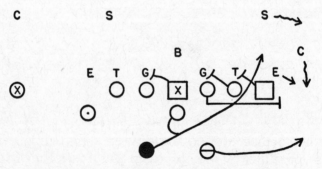

Figure 7.11   Tight Slot Left, 38 Quick Pitch, 24 Dive.

quick-pitch fake. In this case, you may decide to G-block the end and seal down with your tackle and tight end (see Figure 7.11).

There are many alternative pass plays built into the dive series. The basic 32, 34, 21, and 23 dive actions hold the linebackers in place long enough to get the receivers into the short under zones. The quick series and loop series are used primarily when the offense is using the dive series. Below are several plays that are used with a dive action (see Figures 7.12 and 7.13).

The 34 and 23 dive action simulates the veer concept of the triple option. In many cases, the defense adjusts as if the triple

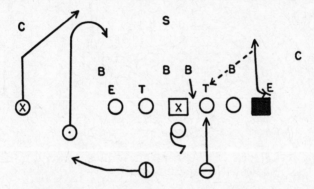

Figure 7.12   Slot Left, 32 Dive Action, 25, Delay 6.

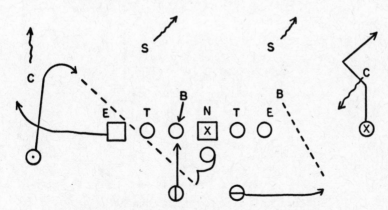

Figure 7.13   Pro Left, 21 Dive Action, 5, Loop, X-Go.

option was being used. There is always some kind of run support coming from the outside, and in the case of the four deep it is either the playside safety or corner. The three-deep zone relies on the outside linebackers to stop the pitch when the quarterback uses the option play.

Passing from the 34 and 23 dive action requires a read from the receivers. The receivers must pick up the action of the supporting defensive backs and run their patterns accordingly.

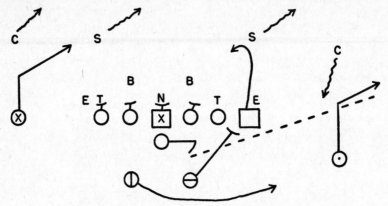

Figure 7.14   Pro Right, 34 Dive Action, 27, Z-Read (Corner Support).

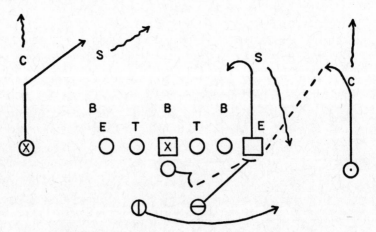

Figure 7.15   Pro Right, 34 Dive Action, 27, Z-Read (Safety Support).

There are only two reads used when facing a four-deep zone. If the corner supports the pitch man, the receiver executes the square out. This puts him in between the safety in the deep third and the corner coming up to support the pitch. If the playside safety is used to shut off the outside, the receiver runs a deep curl pattern between the two safeties (see Figures 7.14 and 7.15).

The three-deep zone is much easier to attack when using the outside dive action. The linebackers pursue in a flat lateral direction expecting the triple option. Their precise angles are toward the play and in a forward direction. This allows the quarterback to pick out any receiver over the middle to the playside. One of the best formations for this type of play is the tight slot (see Figure 7.16).

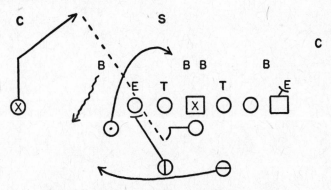

Figure 7.16   Tight Slot Left, 23 Dive Action, 250.

The quick passing action to set up the dive play gives the offense several combinations for throwing. By faking the quick pass to a receiver and then turning around and giving the ball to the back, the defensive secondary could be lulled to sleep. Sending faking receivers deep after the dive has been faked has a tremendous effect on your scoring capability. Below are two plays that have proven successful over the years (see Figures 7.17 and 7.18).

When motion is used by the halfbacks or flankers, the defense has a tendency to overcompensate to the motion side.

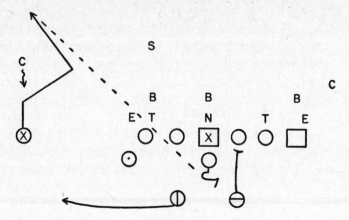

Figure 7.17   Tight Slot Left, 32 Dive Action, X-Pop, Go.

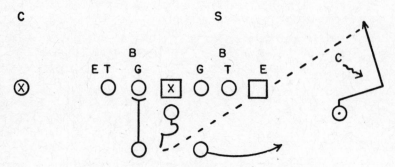

Figure 7.18   Pro Right, 21 Dive Action, Z-Fire, Go.

As the pass is faked to the man in motion and brought back to a running back, the defense reacts as if it were a run. This leaves the under zones uncovered by the linebackers.

There is one specific pass play used when a back goes in motion to set up the dive (see Figure 7.19).

This play has three potential open receivers.

1. Split end: As the playside linebacker moves up to help with the motion receiver, he has moved out of position to cover the split end on his curl pattern.

2. Flankers: Because of the curl pattern by the split end, a pick has been established for the flanker's X pattern.

3. Left halfback: By running the normal 33 dive with motion, the playside linebacker may have been burnt enough times to be guessing that the play will be a run. In this case, he supports the run and lets the motion back go.

As the quarterback fakes the pass to the motion back, he can read the linebacker and defensive corner. This enables him to pick out his open receiver. If the safety assists on the play, a reverse pick is used and the split end executes a 2 pattern off the flankers' 7 pattern pick.

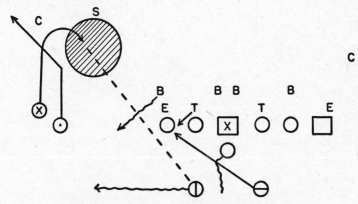

Figure 7.19   Twins Left, L-Odd, 33 Dive Action, 5X0, L-Loop.

THE CROSS-BUCK SERIES

Another key play of the inside ground attack is the cross buck. The cross buck is a very effective misdirection play that forces the defense to react quickly. One of the biggest advantages of this play is that the cross-buck action can be used frequently to set up specific pass patterns.

Within the cross-buck series there are special pass plays that directly involve the backs. As the cross-buck action is used, linebackers often have a tendency to forget about the backfield personnel as receivers. As you will see, the crossing pattern by the backs opens up passes to the backs in the underflats area.

The cross-buck running play is directed into the 1 and 2 holes when normal blocking calls are made. If G-trapping is used, the holes are called one hole wider, so that the trapping guard can kick out the holeman (see Figures 7.20, 7.21, 7.22, and 7.23).

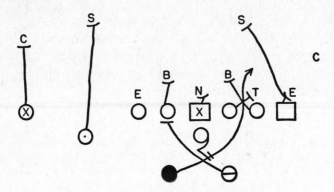

Figure 7.20   Slot Left, 22 Cross Buck.

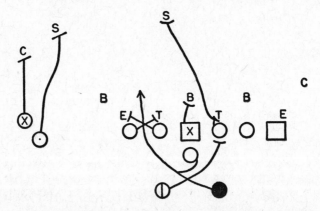

Figure 7.21   Twins Left, 31 Cross Buck.

When executing the cross buck, the quarterback steps to the side of the faking back, who always goes first. Once this fake has been completed, the quarterback reverses, pivots, and hands off to the designated back. Like the delay dive, the ball carrier stays in his stance for one full second before hitting the hole. This gives the quarterback and faking back time to set up their fake.

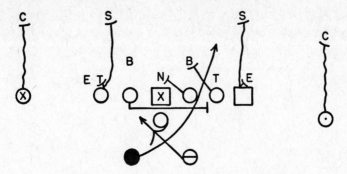

Figure 7.22   Pro Right, 22 Cross Buck, G-Trap.

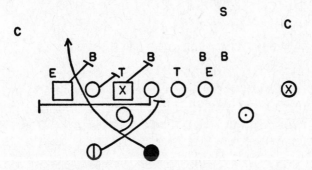

Figure 7.23   Unbalanced Right, 31 Cross Buck, G-Trap.

COUNTERACTION PASSING

There are two major pass plays that involve the backs when using cross-buck action. These plays work most effectively against defenses that use inside linebackers, such as the 6–2, 5–2, and 6–1 alignments.

When facing these defenses, the cross-buck action is directed toward the outside of the formation, into the areas of the 5 and 6 holes. As the play is called, the designated ball carrier goes second and is used as a blocker. The faking back, who normally goes first, fakes a block on the defensive end and continues out into the flats.

The quarterback uses the same faking action as in the 22 and 31 cross buck, however, he now steps at a 45 degree angle toward the backs in order to give a good fake and prepares to set up for the pass (see Figure 7.24).

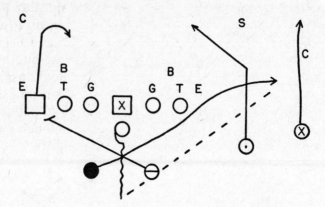

Figure 7.24   Slot Right, 26 Cross Buck Pass, 5X6.

If you face a three-deep, man-to-man technique in the secondary, you may wish to send your flanker or slot man in motion away from the cross-buck pass to pull the safety out of position.

The 35 cross-buck pass is the mirror passing play in this series. In this play, the number 2 back goes first in the cross-buck action, and the number 3 back fakes a block on the defensive end before releasing into the flats (see Figure 7.25).

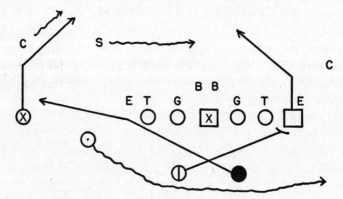

Figure 7.25   Slot Left, Z-Even, 35 Cross Buck Pass, 2, Loop, X.

As shown in Figure 7.25, secondary responsibilities have to be changed to cover the four possible receivers: the split and tight ends, flanker, and halfback. This basic play has the advantage of having at least one receiver open on every play.

In adjusting to this, defensive ends have been used in defending the motion man as well as the cross-buck receiver in a man-to-man technique. By doing this, the offense can strike deep quickly, as well a flare a back to the tight-end side off the cross-buck action. The tight end runs an X-go pattern, and the left halfback flares once he has seen the defensive end to his side pull out with the motion man (see Figure 7.26).

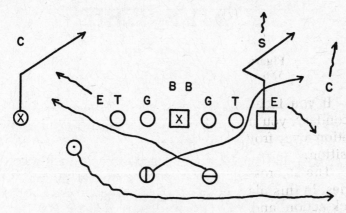

Figure 7.26   Slot Left, Z-Even, 35 Cross Buck Pass, 2, Loop, X-Go, L-Flare.

As the play is executed, the quarterback reads the corner to the strong side. With additional support in the flats by the defensive end, the corner takes the tight end deep. This leaves an opening between the defensive end and defensive corner for the flare receiver.

8

MISDIRECTING THE DEFENSE
WITH THE INSIDE
COUNTER SERIES

The inside counterplay is one of the most effective plays used in high school football today. Like the dive play, it can be executed quickly and with precision.

In the pro-T attack, there are two basic inside counterplays. The 22 and 31 inside counters supply the pro-T with both an inside ground game as well as a stable base for its many play-action passes.

When executing the counter series, the quarterback reverse pivots away from the designated hole. His major role is to fake the sweep pitch to the trailing halfback. As the quarterback continues this play, he turns to the inside and hands off to the ball carrier. Once this is completed, he runs parallel along the line of scrimmage to the side of the play. The designated ball carrier remains in his stance for one full second as the ball is faked to the sweeping back by the quarterback. This gives the line adequate time to set up the blocking (see Figures 8.1 and 8.2).

COUNTERACTION PASSING

As in most base plays, the counter also has a number of variations that can be executed from the same action.

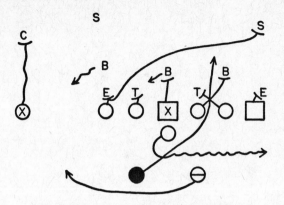

Figure 8.1 Pro Right, 22 Counter.

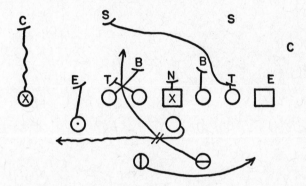

Figure 8.2 Tight Slot Left, 31 Counter.

When the normal base counter has been used several times, the faking back becomes no more than a decoy as he carries out his fake. The defensive end, or linebacker, eventually fails to pick this back up in the flats area, as the counter has effectively been used to hold the defense in their basic positions. Once the quarterback has been informed by the faking back that he is no longer being covered, the next play will be the counteraction, with the pass going to the faking back (see Figure 8.3).

In order to stop this play, the defensive end or linebacker is used to pick up the looping back. The linebacker can provide better coverage of the loop receiver than the defensive end. As the linebacker moves to the outside to key the looping back in a

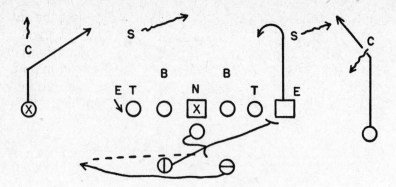

Figure 8.3   Pro Right, 31 Counteraction Pass, 27X.

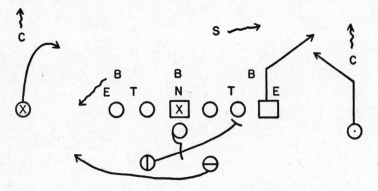

Figure 8.4   Pro Right, 22 Counteraction, 52X.

man-to-man technique, the short curl zone to the split end side opens (see Figure 8.4).

The counter series consists of two basic plays, the counter and the counterpass. With the addition of motion, there are several other plays that develop from the counteraction. These plays are designed for, and against the aggressive linebacker who causes problems on all outside plays.

This play is an adaptation of the 22 and 31 inside counter. To stop outside run support by the outside linebacker, a pop pattern is used by the split end to pick the linebacker and prevent him from following the motion man. As the flanker goes in motion, he continues to turn upfield and blocks the outside defensive back. As the motion man approaches the defensive corner, he must attempt to block him from the outside in and keep position on the corner so that he is between the defender and the receiving halfback. If the defensive corner supports the screen by the halfback before the motion man can pick him up, the motion man returns to the huddle and informs the quarterback that he isn't being picked up.

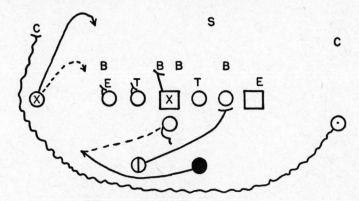

Figure 8.5   Pro Right, Z-Odd, 22 Counteraction Halfback Screen, Pop, X, 0.

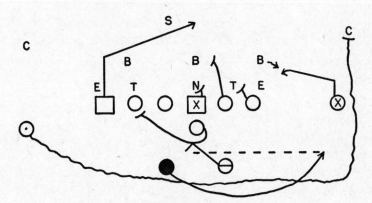

Figure 8.6   Pro Left, Z-Even, 31 Counteraction Halfback Screen, 0, 2, Pop.

To illustrate this, Figures 8.5 and 8.6 give you an idea of how the halfback screen from the counteraction can be executed. Figures 8.7 and 8.8 show how a deep pass can develop once the defensive corner has committed himself too early.

In order to deceive the defensive backs into supporting the screen, the quarterback must take a long look at the screen back so that the motion man has time to execute his deep pattern.

By consistently sticking to the counterseries, a defensive adjustment is made in order to bring another defender into the area of the motion man and screening back.

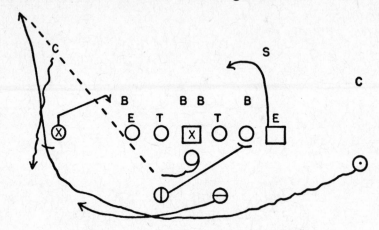

Figure 8.7   Pro Right, Z-Odd, 22 Counteraction, Pop, X, 7.

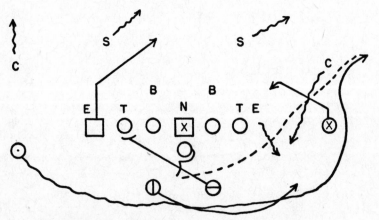

Figure 8.8   Pro Left, Z-Even, 31 Counteraction, 2, 2, Pop.

To support the deep third (slanting receivers and screening halfback) the safety has to be prerotated into the short flats area. By doing this, the defense has the deep thirds covered, so the motion man is not open deep. The safety is able to come up quickly and prevent the halfback from getting big yardage, and the playside linebacker is able to handle his hook zone (see Figure 8.9). This adjustment by the defense adequately hampers the results of the counteraction with motion to the playside.

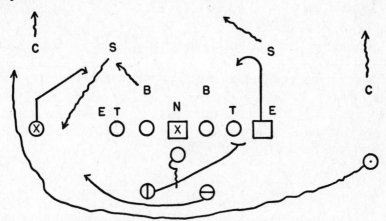

Figure 8.9   Defensive Adjustment Vs. Counterseries Passing.

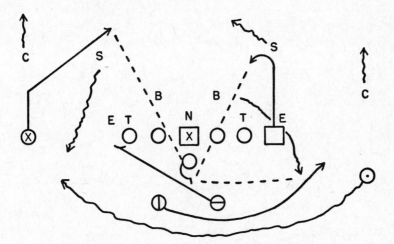

Figure 8.10   Pro Right, Z-Odd, 31 Counterpass, 2, Delay-7, Loop.

To compensate for this adjustment, motion is used as a decoy to force the secondary into rotating away from the next series of plays. The counteraction is used in its normal series, except the motion man is now sent away from the play (see Figure 8.10).

By supporting the motion side with the safety, the defense has allowed the split end to split the zones with a 2 pattern. The defensive corner to the looping back's side has rotated into the deep third and taken himself out of position to cover the back coming out of the backfield to his side. If the linebacker to the back's side is playing the looping halfback in a man-to-man technique, the tight end is given the delay-7 call. The tight end must first block the defensive end hard to the outside before releasing. This gives the quarterback time to set up properly, plus gives the linebacker time to move out of his zone if he is picking up the looping left halfback.

COUNTERACTION OPTION SERIES

At this point, the defensive secondary realizes that a pre-determined rotation may not be the answer to stopping the counterpassing series. In order to cover all areas within this phase of the attack, a total defensive change has to be made. The defense, however, must keep the four defensive backs in the secondary and change to a three linebacker set. The 4–3 defense is probably the most effective in covering both short flats and

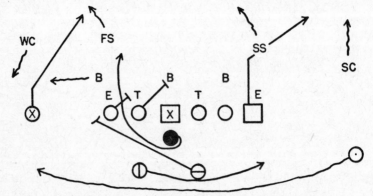

Figure 8.11   Quarterback Option Keep—Seal Blocking with an H-Block Kick Out on the Defensive End.

the deep passing zones. As the adjustment is made by the defense, the offense adds its option attack to the counter series. When running the option, you must make sure that the motion is used away from the looping back in the counter series. This puts two receivers in the flats on both sides of the formation and forces the outside linebackers into clearing their areas as they pick up their offensive players. The play to be executed first is the pro right, Z-odd, 33 counteroption keep, 22 X (see Figure 8.11).

Because of containment by the outside linebacker, the off-tackle holes are vulnerable to the quarterback keep on the option series. The H-block call added to the 33 counter tells the line to seal block, and that the counterback is kicking out the end in an H-block technique. In order to hold the free safety from supporting the quarterback keep, a post pattern is run by the split end. From this option series, the normal counter to the 3 hole can be executed with switch blocking to the weak side of the formation. This is successful if the outside linebacker contains the motion man. The outside linebacker may choose to stay in tight and protect the counter hole or take the quarterback on the keeper. This enables the quarterback to pitch the ball to the motion man (see Figures 8.12 and 8.13).

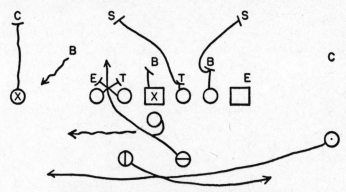

Figure 8.12   Pro Right, Z-Odd, 33 Counter.

Although the counter series is a simple one, it has numerous variations which include the option keep by the quarterback, pitch to the man in motion, and the basic option give. This series is basically an attack within the pro-T and can be used effectively against any defense.

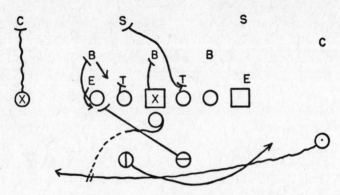

Figure 8.13 Pro Right, Z-Odd, 33 Counterop-tion Pitch.

The four-deep zone is more difficult to throw deep against, but it is more susceptible to the counteroption series. The three-deep zone may have enough defenders up front to stop the basic counterplay and option series, but this type of defense gives up the deep pass patterns to the counteraction passing series.

9

DEVELOPING THE BIG PLAY WITH THE OUTSIDE COUNTER SERIES

The outside counter series uses a wider variety of formations than the inside counter series. This series has the capability of attacking any hole from end to end.

The base play in the counter series is the 45 and 46 counter. The flanker executes the play. In the 45 and 46 counter, both the right and left halfbacks are used as decoys with sweep action away from the counterhole. The quarterback reverse pivots out of his stance and fakes a sweep pitch to the two halfbacks. Then he turns 90 degrees and hands off inside to the flanker or

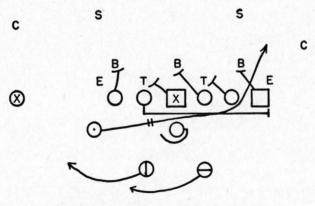

Figure 9.1   Tight Slot Left, 46 Counter.

151

counter ball carrier. Since misdirection action is being used, the G-trap block, along with the seal block, is applied by the offensive line.

The counter series is generally run from a tight slot, although motion may be used to put the ball carrier in a better position to receive the direct handoff from the quarterback. To illustrate the base counter, two examples are given. The first is from a tight slot and the other is the counterplay with motion action (see Figures 9.1 and 9.2).

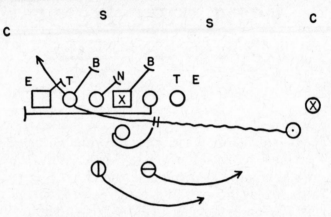

Figure 9.2   Twins Right, Z-Odd, 45 Counter.

There are many other counters from the 45 and 46 series that are executed from a wide variety of formations. Below are four examples showing the versatility of this play. In this series,

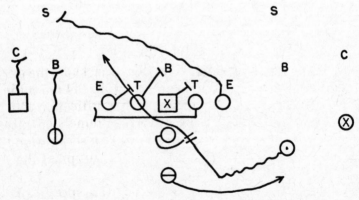

Figure 9.3   Twins Right, Z-Odd, 43 Counter.

the attack hole may vary depending on the defensive alignment (see Figures 9.3, 9.4, 9.5, and 9.6).

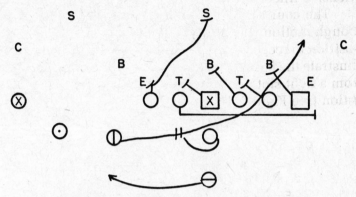

Figure 9.4   Trips Left, L-Even, 26 Counter.

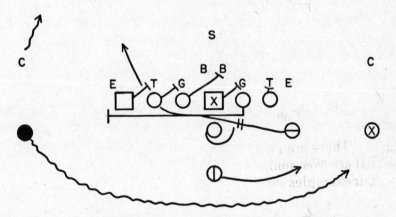

Figure 9.5   Pro Left, Tight Slot Right, Z-Even, 35 Counter.

Note that the number 2 and number 3 backs are the primary ball carriers. You may notice that in Figure 9.4 the number 2 back was sent in motion by using his identification letter.

The counterplay has proven to be extremely effective because it spreads out the defense. The counter series, along with its many variations of the base play, has supplied the pro-T offense with numerous play-action passes.

Like many plays in this offense, there are specific plays set up strictly for the halfbacks.

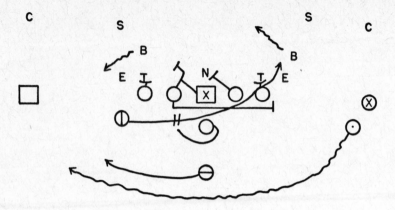

Figure 9.6   Twins Right, Tight Slot Left, Z-Odd, 26 Counter.

COUNTERACTION SHORT PASSING GAME

There are two basic plays that are executed from the counteraction. By successfully running the counter, the defense has a tendency to neglect the two faking backs coming out of the backfield away from the counter. This sets up the loop pass to one back, with the other back blocking lead.

As the fake is executed by the quarterback and the two halfbacks, the playside back picks up the first defender to his side. This defender may be a defensive end, linebacker, or defensive back (see Figures 9.7 and 9.8).

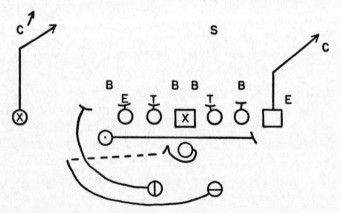

Figure 9.7   Tight Slot Left, 46 Counteraction, Halfback Pass, 202.

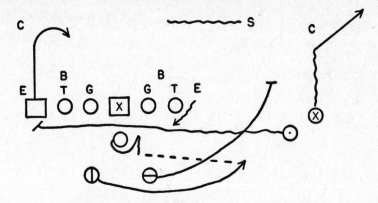

Figure 9.8   Twins Right, Z-Odd, 45 Counteraction, Halfback Pass, 502.

In the halfback pass play there is no G-trap block used. Play-action protection by the line is applied to this play.

While using the counteraction, the counterback may be in a set position or put into the play with the use of motion. By showing pass out of the counteraction, the counterback, or flanker, is often uncovered as he continues his fake into the flats. His pattern is chosen by the type of pass rush coming from the defensive end on the counterside. As the tight end releases downfield, the defensive end is unguarded by the offensive line. He rushes the passer without regard to his backside re-

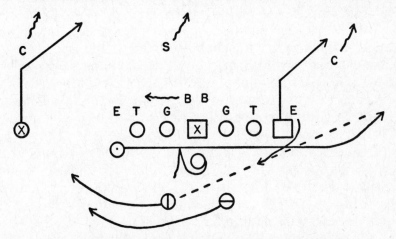

Figure 9.9   Tight Slot Left, 46 Counteraction, 2, Loop, 2.

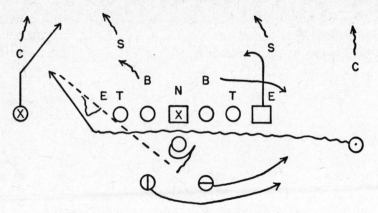

Figure 9.10   Pro Right, Z-Odd, 45 Counteraction, 2, 7, Loop.

sponsibility. This mistake by the defensive end enables the counterback to run directly past the defensive end and get open in the short under zone. The defensive end, who sticks with the counterback, has to be taken upfield in order to shake his coverage. Figures 9.9 and 9.10 illustrate how this play is affected by the read on the defensive end.

The counteraction holds the secondary in position so that deep patterns can be executed. This action also holds the linebackers in their original positions long enough to allow the quarterback to set up. This play is extremely effective against defenses that use two inside linebackers. The key to its success is the ability of the quarterback to give a head fake away from the primary receivers long enough to enable the receiver to get clear of the short coverage. The quarterback should always look away as long as possible before turning back to his main target.

The effectiveness of this play may force the defense to adjust by adding more outside run support or pass coverage. There is a possibility that the defense may switch to a 4–3 or 4–4 to give added linebacker support. When this change is made the tight ends become very important. As motion is used, the two backs leave the backfield and the outside linebackers are expected to pick them up. This opens up a natural seam for the tight end, who executes a delay shoot.

In order to get the full potential from this play, the quarterback must look to both the motion man and faking backs before

coming back to the tight end. By looking at the outside receivers, the linebackers are drawn out of their hook zones as
they pick up the outside receivers, leaving the middle area
unguarded (see Figures 9.11 and 9.12).

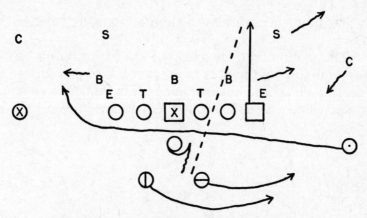

Figure 9.11   Pro Right, Z-Odd, 45 Counteraction, Y-Delay Shoot.

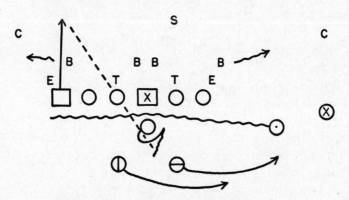

Figure 9.12   Slot Right, Z-Odd, 45 Counteraction, Y-Delay Shoot.

The combination of counterpassing to the halfback, motion receiver, and tight end makes the defense aware of the
outside perimeter. To take advantage of this adjustment by the
defense, an inside counterplay is executed by the motion receiver. The outside linebackers are now aware of the passes that
have been thrown to the motion receiver and backs moving out

of the backfield. Their overcompensating causes a crease to be formed in the off-tackle area.

OPTIONAL COUNTER SERIES

This type of counter is a simulation using cross-buck action.

The motion man goes behind the two running backs instead of in front of them, as in the normal counter series. As he is positioned behind the near back to his side, he accelerates to the designated hole. The quarterback steps toward the blast

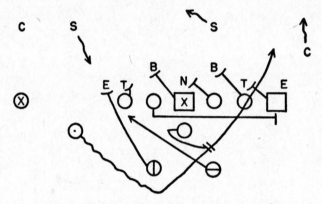

Figure 9.13   Slot Left, Z-Even, 33 Blast Action, 46 Counter (G-Trap).

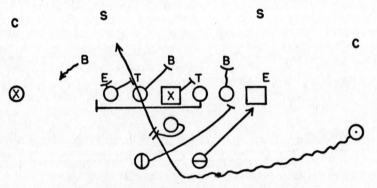

Figure 9.14   Pro Right, Z-Odd, 24 Blast Action, 43 Counter (G-Trap).

hole and fakes to the action back. Then he reverses, pivots, and hands off to the counter ball carrier (see Figures 9.13 and 9.14).

The counter off the blast action may require the use of a G-trap block. If the linebackers are overly aggressive and chase the action, normal blocking calls are applied.

Optional Counter Series Passing

When using the blast action to set up the counter, the faking blast backs are coached to read the reaction of the defensive end and linebacker to the faking side. These reads may set up another play that is frequently used from these two examples shown above.

The faking backs must determine which flare back can get into the flats with the least amount of resistance from the defensive end. This information is given to the quarterback.

This particular play is effective to either the strong or weak side of the formation, and there is the possibility that the counterman may also be able to sneak into the flats once his fake has been carried out. Below are four illustrations showing the use of this play. Figures 9.15 and 9.16 show the counterback used as a blocker on the weak side. Figures 9.17 and 9.18 illustrate his effectiveness as he is able to sneak into the flats undetected.

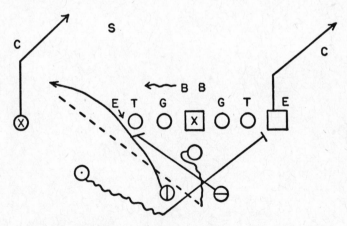

Figure 9.15   Slot Left, Z-Even, 33 Blast Action, 46 Counter, 202, L-Flare.

The versatility of the counter series is limitless. It has the capability of controlling both the linebacking as well as secondary rotations. The use of a monster adds even more frustration to the overall defense of this series.

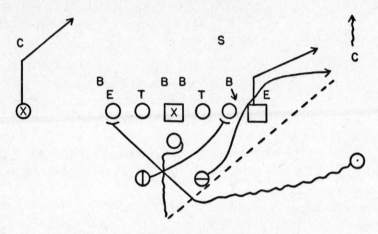

Figure 9.16   Pro Right, Z-Odd, 24 Blast Action, 43 Counter, 220, R-Flare.

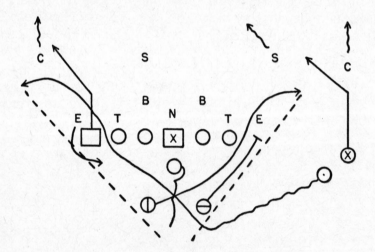

Figure 9.17   Twins Right, Z-Odd, 24 Blast Action, 45 Counter, X-Flare, L-Flare.

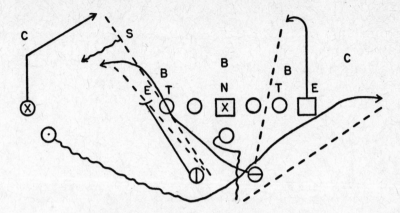

Figure 9.18   Twins Left, Z-Even, 33 Blast Action, 46 Counter, 2 Flare, 7, R-Flare. (There are four possible receivers open on this pattern.)

10

THE VERSATILITY OF THE OUTSIDE GAME

The off-tackle blast series, power sweep, and quick pitch are more than just three basic types of plays. The versatility and strategy of these plays are discussed in this chapter.

BLAST SERIES

Because of its simplicity, quick-hitting effect, and the power generated at the hole, the blast series became one of the most widely used plays in the pro-T attack. To stop this play, the defense is forced to send as many defenders into the hole area as possible. This defensive commitment allows the off-tackle play to be used with an option adaptation, as well as an excellent play-action passing diversion.

To begin with, the basic blast play is discussed. Recalling halfback blocking, the blast call indicates that a halfback is used as a lead blocker. The H-block and G-block alter his blocking pattern, but this play always has a halfback lead.

In the blast series, the 24 and 33 blast are the base plays. Action from the quarterback is simple: He merely reverse pivots away from the play and hands off to the designated ball carrier. In order to add future plays, the quarterback follows down the line of scrimmage once he has handed off. Figures 10.1 thru

10.6 show how the 24 and 33 blast plays can be executed. The G-block and H-block adjustments can be used if needed.

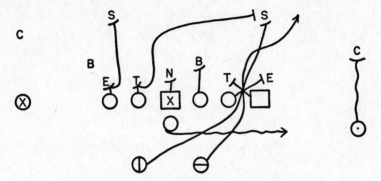

Figure 10.1   Pro Right, 24 Blast (Switch Block at Hole).

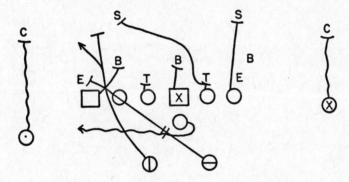

Figure 10.2   Pro Left, 33 Blast (Fold Block at Hole).

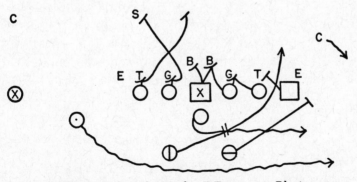

Figure 10.3   Slot Left, Z-Even, 24 Blast, H-Block.

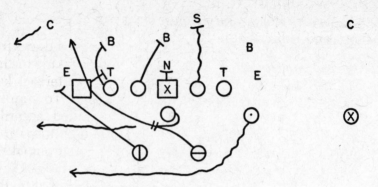

Figure 10.4   Tight Slot Right, Z-Odd, 33 Blast, H-Block.

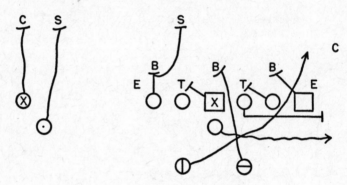

Figure 10.5   Twins Left, 24 Blast, G-Block.

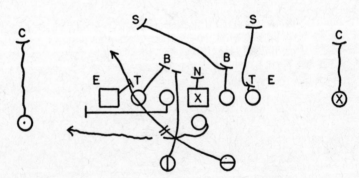

Figure 10.6   Pro Left, 33 Blast, G-Block.

The continuous action by the quarterback in the follow through of this play opens up several variations to the 24 and 33 blast.

Blast Series Option Game

Because of the attention that the ball carrier draws from the defense, an option series can be executed by faking the handoff to the primary ball carrier and having the quarterback keep the ball or pitch it to the trailing motion man. To simplify the blocking used, the plays are predetermined according to whether the quarterback keeps the ball or pitches it. If the quarterback keep is used, normal blocking up front takes place as if the blast play has been called. The quarterback fakes the handoff to the designated ball carrier and follows him through the hole (see Figures 10.7 and 10.8).

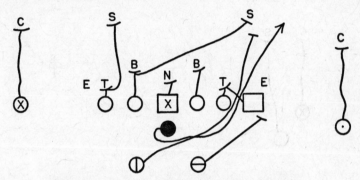

Figure 10.7 Pro Right, 24 Blast, H-Block Keep.

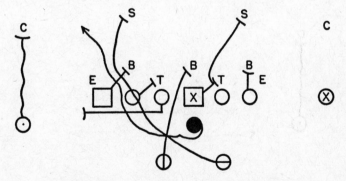

Figure 10.8 Pro Left, 33 Blast, G-Block Keep.

By continuously hitting the same hole over and over again with the blast series, or quarterback keep, the defense begins to tighten up the perimeter in defense of the off-tackle hole.

When using the pitch on the strong side, the tight end makes aggressive contact on the defensive end. Then he releases on the first defender to his outside. Normally this is a defensive corner back, but it could also be a rotating safety who is responsible for the flats area. Both backs attack the designated hole in an H-block fashion. This cuts down on linebacker support to the pitch. The quarterback reverse pivots and fakes a handoff to the faking back. Then he continues down the line until he sees the commitment of the defensive end, at which time he pitches (see Figures 10.9 and 10.10).

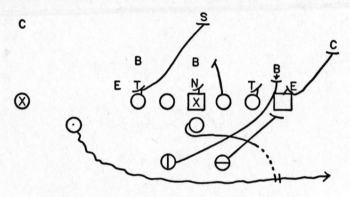

Figure 10.9 Slot Left, Z-Even, 24 Blast, H-Block Pitch.

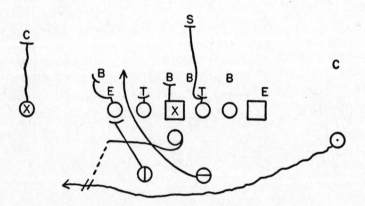

Figure 10.10 Pro Right, Z-Odd, 33 Blast, H-Block Pitch.

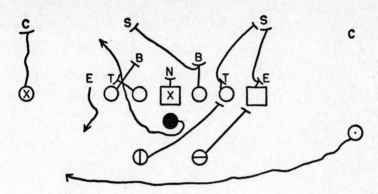

Figure 10.11 Pro Right, Z-Odd, 24 Blast, Bootleg Keep.

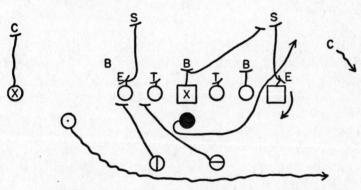

Figure 10.12 Slot Left, Z-Even, 33 Blast, Bootleg Keep.

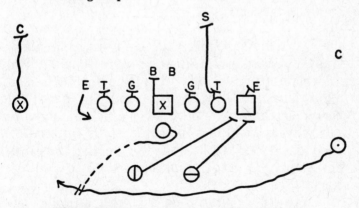

Figure 10.13 Pro Right, Z-Odd, 24 Blast, Bootleg Pitch.

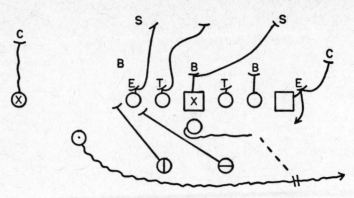

Figure 10.14 Slot Left, Z-Even, 33 Blast, Bootleg Pitch.

By attacking the off-tackle hole with the blast option pitch and quarterback keep, the defense becomes very protective of that area. To offset this, the offense uses the bootleg phase of the off-tackle series. In this play, both backs attack the off-tackle hole away from the bootleg action. The quarterback pivots to the side that the backs are attacking and continues his bootleg down the line. Both the bootleg keeper and pitch to the motion man are blocked the same as the blast keeper and blast option pitch (see Figures 10.11 thru 10.14).

Blast Series Passing

The off-tackle series uses basically the same play-action passes as those used in the outside counterattack. When using these play-action passes, you will find that in most cases at least two of the four possible receivers are open. To identify the four receivers we diagram one basic play-action pass and discuss the capability of each possible receiver. In Figure 10.15, the play pro right, Z-odd, 24 blast action, bootleg pass is used.

The bootleg pass call by the quarterback was not given with a specific, primary receiver. Very few high school quarterbacks have the capability of reading the entire defensive alignment and their responsibilities. This is why one primary receiver is selected out of the four possibilities. Each receiver is

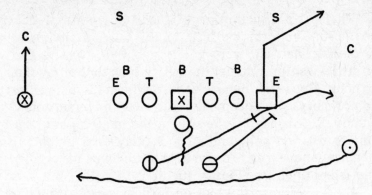

Figure 10.15 Blast Action with Four Possible
Receivers.

chosen through verbal communication between the quarterback and the man himself. In other words, if the motion man has
not been picked up by the outside linebacker the motion man
informs the quarterback. The next play is a pass to the flanker,
or we run the same action several times and wait until the
defense has picked him up and see how their total defensive
adjustment has changed to stop the motion. This information is
used to set up further plays. Rather than discuss all the play-
action passes in detail, Figures 10.16 thru 10.20 illustrate those
plays. Each play is called as it would be in the game. The
strategy behind the play is also explained.

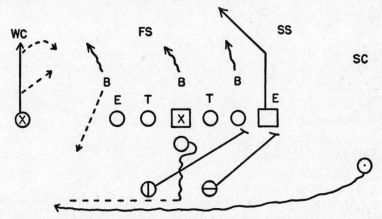

Figure 10.16 Pro Right, Z-Odd, 24 Blast Action, Z-Loop.

The first play-action pass isolates the motion man. If no outside run support picks him up, the ball is thrown to him. If the motion man is a very good open field runner, and you definitely want him to get the ball, a pick pattern by the split end could be used. When isolating on the motion man, the split end normally runs a deep pattern to clear the under zone. With an active linebacker on the side of the motion pass, you may want to use the split end in a 3-delay or 5 pattern. If the linebacker moves out to cover the motion man, his hook or curl zone is left open (see Figure 10.16).

By throwing to the motion man at various times in the game, both the outside linebacker and defensive back begin to concentrate on the flanker. This enables the split end to run a pattern in which the go call adjustment is used.

Of all passing plays, this sequence between the quarterback and split end has been used in 23 percent of all passing plays. If the corner back stays deep and covers the split end, the motion man is open in the flats. If the corner supports the flats, the split end is open deep. As you can see, the corner is wrong no matter what he does (see Figure 10.17).

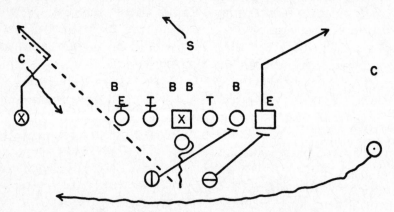

Figure 10.17   Pro Right, Z-Odd, 24 Blast Action, 2-Go, 2, Loop.

A typical situation is one in which the defensive corner to the motion side stays in the deep third and the linebacker takes the motion man. Support in the hook and curl area comes from the free safety. By pulling the linebacker out of the number 3 hole, a simple cross buck play keeps the defense honest (see Figure 10.18).

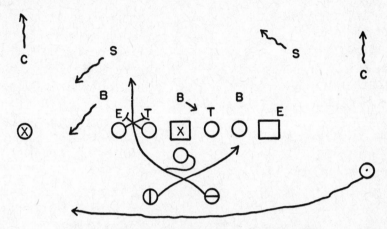

Figure 10.18   Cross Buck Action Used to Offset Linebacker Support on the Motion Man.

The 24 blast action, or L or R flare, is extremely effective against the three-deep, man-to-man defenses in which the defensive corners chase the motion man. It can also be used against the three- and four-deep zone coverages, if the tight end runs a deep 2 or X on the pro side. By doing this, the tight end drives the corner deep and out of the play. This enables the flare back to sneak into the flats without heavy pass coverage in the under zone.

The flare pass is set up by throwing to the motion side several times before coming back with the flare pass. As the flare pass is used, the quarterback should look to the motion man before throwing to the flare back. This holds the flare side linebacker in long enough to enable the back to sneak out unnoticed (see Figure 10.19).

If the weak side defensive ends puts on the type of pass rush that shuts down this play, the motion man could be used to block the defensive end. This would not have to be part of the call, but merely a verbal command by the quarterback in the huddle.

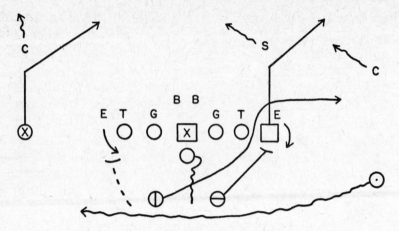

Figure 10.19   Pro Right, Z-Odd, 24 Blast Action, L-Flare, 2, 2, Loop.

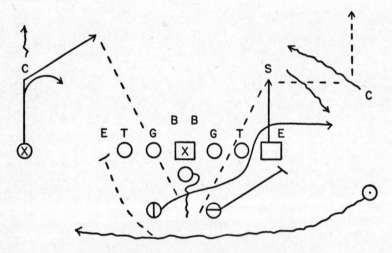

Figure 10.20   Pro Right, Z-Odd, 24 Blast Action, 2, Delay Shoot, Loop, L-Flare.

The last phase of this series is the pass to the tight end. Positioning of the outside linebacker indicates the type of pattern that would be left available to the tight end. These patterns vary from the delay shoot to the 3-go. The split end should know where the safety is playing, and a 6 pattern could be used if the safety is rotating prematurely to the motion side. The safety's rotation is discussed between the quarterback, split end, and tight end. When the tight end is isolated as the primary receiver, the flanker has to be used to block the weak side.

Assuming that the safety is supporting the flare back out of the backfield and the corner is following the motion man in a man-to-man technique, we would want the tight end to get the ball as soon as possible so that he could make as many yards as possible. If the quarterback throws the long pass, the defender, who is following the motion, may be able to recover in time to bat the ball down or, even worse, make an interception (see Figure 10.20).

This covers all the play-action passes in the off-tackle series. All patterns can be set up by waiting for the defense to make commitments that allow you to work on those areas left open.

POWER SWEEP AND QUICK PITCH SERIES

You may be one of those coaches who have athletes who stand still faster than most halfbacks run. If you are that fortunate, you will be able to use the power sweep and quick pitch series.

In the power sweep series, all line blocking is predetermined. You may remember that the power call requires both offensive guards to pull in the direction of the play, and the

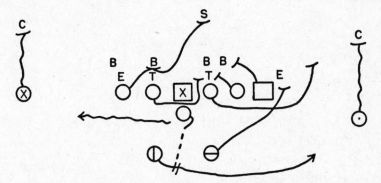

Figure 10.21   Pro Right, 28 Power Sweep.

playside halfback to block the defensive end. The power sweep series has two base plays. These are the 28 and 37 power sweep. The action used by the quarterback is a reverse pivot to the side of the play and a toss action to the designated ball carrier. After the toss, he continues along the line of scrimmage in a bootleg action, running in the opposite direction of the play itself (see Figures 10.21 and 10.22).

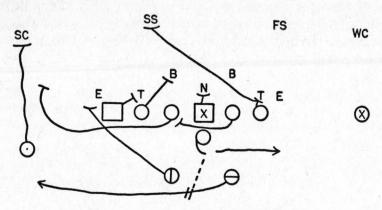

Figure 10.22   Pro Left, 37 Power Sweep.

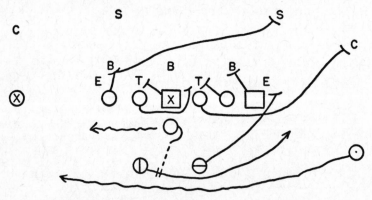

Figure 10.23   Pro Right, Z-Odd, 28 Power Sweep.

When power sweep action is used and both guards are pulling, seal blocking is used by the remainder of the line. The outside receiver on the playside base blocks the outside corner. If motion runs away from the power sweep side, the offensive lead guard blocks the outside corner on the playside (see Figure 10.23).

The base power sweep series can be executed from many formations. Motion may have to be used to put the ball carrier in the proper position for the toss handoff. To show several examples of the variations of the sweep series, Figures 10.24 thru 10.27 illustrate the same play from four different looks. These plays run to the right only (see Figures 10.24 thru 10.27).

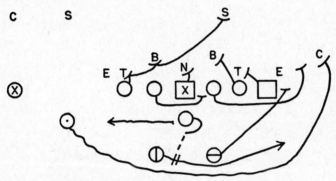

Figure 10.24   Slot Left, Z-Even, 28 Power Sweep.

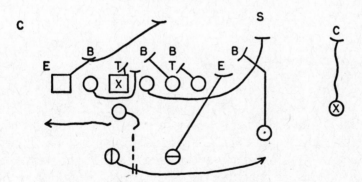

Figure 10.25   Unbalanced Right, Rip, 28 Power Sweep.

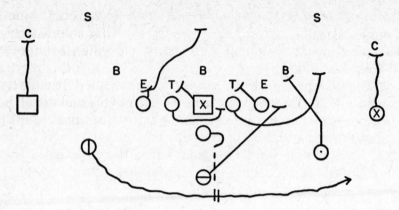

Figure 10.26   Double Slot Right, L-Even, 28 Power Sweep.

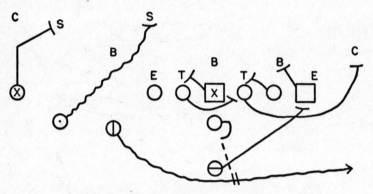

Figure 10.27   Trips Left, L-Even, 28 Power Sweep.

Power Sweep Option Series

Within the power sweep series, there is also a bootleg option and bootleg keep by the quarterback. By looking at Figures 10.28 and 10.29, you can see through the off-tackle examples how these plays are executed. Illustrations 10.28 and 10.29 give you the basic view of each play. The bootleg option and keep are also executed out of the same formations as those diagrammed in Figures 10.24 thru 10.27.

As you look at Figure 10.28, you will see that the two offensive guards still pull to their right. They pull and block the backside pursuit.

The bootleg option keep in Figure 10.29 requires normal blocking calls up front, since there is a designated ball carrier. The guards do not pull in this case, and the offense relies on the backfield deception to set up the play. Against this particular defense, the 5–3, a switch call, is used on the defensive tackle and end. We are assuming that the outside linebacker will move with the motion man, thus allowing the quarterback to split the crease without being picked up.

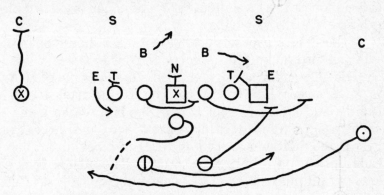

Figure 10.28 Pro Right, Z-Odd, 28 Power Sweep, Bootleg Pitch.

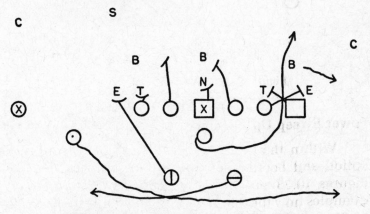

Figure 10.29 Slot Left, Z-Even, 37 Power Sweep, Bootleg Keep.

Power Sweep Passing

In the play-action phase of this series, there are several very good plays that can be executed through the sweep series

action. Two plays out of this series are identical to those used in
Figures 10.13 and 10.14. Those two play-action passes involve
the split end and tight end. The same play action can be used
out of the 28 and 37 power sweep series, and the keys used to set
up those plays are identical in the sweep series.

The play-action passes involving the backs are used to
work on the defensive corner. These plays can be run out of any
formation using the backs in the backfield. When running these
plays out of the pro formation, the motion man is used to block
the weak side defensive end.

If the slot formation is used, the flanker should be in tight
so he can also pick up the weak side pass rushes.

The play-action series to the backs is a two-fold play. As in
the power sweep, the playside back blocks the defensive end to
his side, and the other back carries the ball. When using the
power sweep action passes to the backs, the playside back runs
towards the tight end as if he is going to block him. Then he
heads upfield on a deep flare pattern. The offside back still
loops out into the flats as if he is carrying the ball (see Figure
10.30).

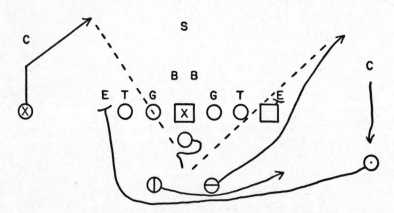

Figure 10.30   Pro Right, Z-Odd, 28 Power
Sweep Action, 200, R-Flare.

Because the play is isolating directly on the two backs, the
tight end stays in and blocks. The quarterback, after carrying

out his fake, keys the outside corner to see what his reaction will be. If he goes deep on the right halfback, the ball is thrown to the loop receiver. If the corner commits himself to the loop receiver, the pass is thrown deep, to the flare receiver. To prevent the safety from picking up the deep flare man the split end runs a 2 pattern. If the safety does pick up the flare man, we run the same action and go deep to the split end. When using this play against the three-man secondary, it has resulted in a bigger gain or a touchdown. Very few times has the safety moved over in time to help the corner on this play. This is another case where the defensive corner is wrong, no matter what he does.

The power sweep series can be used very effectively, both in running and passing. We have not been that fortunate in having tremendous speed in the backfield, but somehow the power sweep series, with its running and passing ability, has helped our offense in key situations. For those coaches who have above-average speed every year, this could be one of your best play series.

QUICK PITCH SERIES

This is also one of those series that requires good speed by the backs. We do not use the quick pitch very often, but two plays out of its action may be even more beneficial than the quick pitch itself. Before we get into those plays, the quick pitch should be covered.

In the quick pitch series there is the 38 and 23 quick pitch. In this play, the playside tackle pulls in the direction of the hole. The tight end tries to hook the defensive end long enough to allow the offensive tackle to turn the corner. As in most outside plays, the quarterback reverse pivots and tosses to the playside back. Once he has done this, he shuffles down the line of scrimmage in the direction of the outside hole. The other back hits the off-tackle hole and picks up the defensive tackle. Since these plays are executed to the 7 and 8 holes, the outside receivers base block the defense corners to the inside (see Figures 10.31 and 10.32).

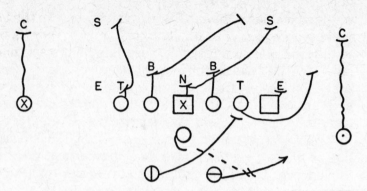

Figure 10.31   Pro Right, 38 Quick Pitch.

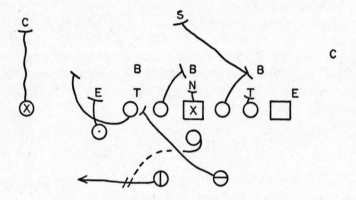

Figure 10.32   Tight Slot Left, 27 Quick Pitch.

Quick Pitch Influence

By running this play, the outside linebackers and defensive ends have a tendency to fight very hard ⁺o their outside. This sets up one of the best plays in this series. To show how splits can help you set up a play, the tight end or flanker keeps taking splits about 6 inches wider every time this play is executed. Eventually the defensive end will think that every time a bigger split is taken the quick pitch play will be used. When the time is right, the play is changed so that the second back, who normally blocks the defensive tackle, gets the ball. When this play is called, normal blocking calls are used. As the quarterback reverse pivots and gets ready to pitch out, he fakes the pitch and holds the ball on a horizonal plane for the far back to take the handoff through a hole that was left open simply because the defense overreacted (see Figures 10.33 and 10.34).

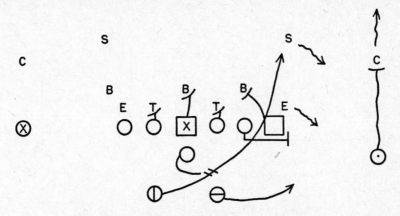

Figure 10.33 Pro Right, 38 Quick Pitch Action, 24 Dive.

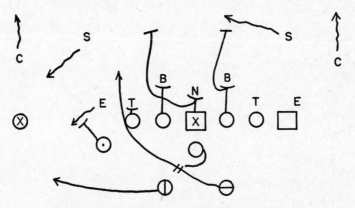

Figure 10.34 Tight Slot Left, 27 Quick Pitch Action, 33 Dive.

The play shown in Figure 10.35 opens up the looping back, if the defensive end starts playing tight to the inside again. In Figure 10.35 you can see that there could possibly be at least two deep receivers open. All play-action passes covered in this chapter open up receivers deep at any time. Because of the play-action effect and the use of the short passing game in the flats, the defense is manipulated at will.

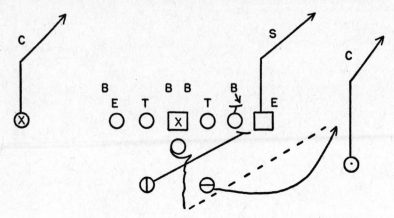

Figure 10.35   Pro Right, 38–24 Action, 222, R-Loop.

11

DRILLS THAT DEVELOP THE PRO-T PERSONNEL

PHILOSOPHY

Our philosophy in drilling is synonymous with the ideas of most coaches. We believe that each drill should meet the needs of each athlete, plus benefit the offensive approach. We use very few drills, but we insist that each drill be conducted with intensity and consistency. Each drill is fundamentally sound and, when properly executed, can teach each athlete exactly how to react in a pressure situation.

With trial and error, these drills have been selected from a large number of basic drills to teach the quarterbacks how to read various types of coverages, condition the receivers to react when a defensive coverage opens up, and instruct the halfbacks and linemen how to outthink their opponents. Drills have a tendency to become boring and repetitious. Adding some spice with a competitive edge stimulates learning and enables the athlete to get in shape without going through the painful and unmotivating experience of running sprints. The following drills will improve the overall performance of the offensive players.

LINE DRILLS

As you read through these drills, note that many of them are used to teach blocking principles rather than blocking techniques. We do spend an adequate amount of time working on the one-on-one blocks and various drills involving the seven-man sled. The main emphasis is directed toward teaching linemen how to mentally beat their opponent.

Screen Blocking Drill—First Stage

Each offensive lineman positions himself in front of a defender. On "ready" all offensive linemen make a false block-ing call. On "set" both the offensive blocker and defender assume a three-point stance. On the first "hut," the offensive lineman fires out making contact with the inside shoulder to the playside hip of the defender. Once contact is made, the blocker slides his body to one side so he becomes positioned at a right angle to the defender. The offensive blocker should make contact as quickly as possible [see Figure 11.1 (a) and (b)].

Figure 11.1(a)   First Contact.

Figure 11.1(b)   Contact After Slide.

Step Back Drill—Stage Two

From stage one, we instruct the defender to step back as soon as the ball is snapped and attempt to push the blocker to the ground with his hands. At the snap, the offensive lineman takes one step forward trying to screen out the defender. As he sees the defender moving backwards, he takes several more steps in order to maintain playside position as he screens out the defender.

This drill should be executed as quickly as possible so that the offensive blocker can make contact with the defender before he is able to push him down. We have found that this phase of the drill teaches the blocker to maintain body control so he fires off the line. It also prevents him from diving after the defender [see Figure 11.2 (a) and (b)].

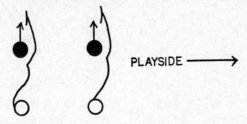

PLAYSIDE ⟶

Figure 11.2(a)   First Step Is a Control Step.

Figure 11.2(b)   Second Step Is a Slide to Contact.

Reaction Drill—Stage Three

Stage three teaches the offensive lineman to react against blitzing, slanting, and defenders who step back during the play. Lining head up on the defender, the offensive blocker fires out with a powerful, but well controlled, first step. Once the offensive blocker has seen how the defender will react, he makes his adjustment in order to screen out his opponent. In screening out the defender, the blockers use the same technique used in Figure 11.2(b) (see Figure 11.3).

PLAYSIDE ⟶

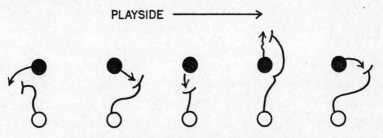

Figure 11.3   React to Defensive Movement.

These three drills have assisted our linemen in developing the skill of getting off the ball quickly while maintaining a good blocking position. By working on these techniques, you will find that your offensive blocker does less diving at the defender and is able to cut off defensive personnel in pursuit of the play.

Call Drill and Step Drill—Stage One

This drill involves a seven-man offensive line and eight defenders who change their defensive alignment on every play. In the case of the 43 or 52, one of the defenders moves out of the play. Once a play is called, the offensive line breaks and sets their normal splits at the line. A coach positioned under the center calls "ready." On "ready," the lineman makes his appropriate blocking calls. On "set," all linemen assume a three-point stance. On "hut," all offensive blockers aggressively charge towards the defenders and make contact. Once contact is made, both the defensive and offensive blockers freeze. The line coach checks the offensive blockers to see if they have maintained a proper blocking technique and if a hole has been created. If you are not satisfied, correct the body positions or angles at which the blocks were made. Then blow a whistle and the line returns to the huddle for the next play.

Call Drill and Read Drill—Stage Two

The call and read drill teaches the offensive linemen to react to shifts and alignment changes by the defense once a play has been called. As the linemen approach the line and make their blocking calls, the defense switches their alignment. The linemen have to block the play, relying solely on their instincts.

Each lineman has to think of the type of block that will be most effective under the circumstances. The number 1 priority is to create a hole at the point of attack. In most cases, you will find that base blocking rules will be applied. Once again, all players freeze on contact so the line coach can make his observation.

Stunt Drill—Stage Three

It is very difficult to teach offensive linemen to pick up the stunt. By practicing against the stunt, you make your linemen aware of this device and improve their ability to pick it up.

As in stage one and two, the offensive linemen approach the line. After the blocking calls are made, the defense aligns itself in position where a stunt is more effective. It is the line's responsibility to pick up the stunts. Through this drill, you can also employ the step-back techniques, slant, twist, loop, and other diversions that may be expected by the defense. Again, all players freeze on contact. Once you have evaluated the blocking techniques used and have seen that all defenders have been blocked, signal the line to return to the huddle.

LINE BLOCKING TECHNIQUES

To teach the basic one-on-one block, we attempt to simulate gamelike conditions. Each defender being blocked has in his possession a portable blocking shield, that he holds waist high and directly in front of him.

Pop Drill—Stage One

This is the first stage in teaching the basic one-on-one block. To assist the linemen in staying low, this drill is conducted under a chute approximately 16 feet long, 3 feet wide, and 4 feet high.

On the snap count, three offensive linemen fire out through the chute and into the blocking shield. Once contact is made, the offensive linemen freeze. The line coach checks to see that contact was made in the hip area of the defender, the lineman's head was positioned to the playside, and that both feet were positioned squarely at the point of contact.

Drive and Screen Drill—Stage Two

The drive drill allows the offensive blocker to take two additional steps after contact has been made. These steps are used to position the offensive lineman to the playside of the defender.

Block Drill—Stage Three

As in the previous two drills, the offensive lineman fires out of his stance in the direction of the defender. When the lineman has cleared the chute and starts his initial block, the defender moves to his right or left and attempts to throw the blocker off. This teaches the offensive lineman to control his charge and regain his body position.

Control Drill—Stage Four

The linemen fire out through the chute and make contact with the air pack. Once contact is made, the defender backs up and weaves from one side to the other. As the defender is doing this, the offensive lineman must maintain his blocking position and stay with the defender.

Spin and Hit Drill

The spin and hit drill teaches the offensive lineman to react as quickly as possible and still remain in a good blocking position. The offensive lineman is in a two-point stance with his back to a defender who is positioned 3 yards away. On your whistle, the offensive lineman turns around as quickly as possible and hits the defender squarely. The defender may run to either side of the blocker or stay right in front of him as he is making contact. When executing this drill, the offensive lineman must always maintain control on the playside, which is given by you (see Figure 11.4).

Figure 11.4   Hit and Control Playside Advantage.

G-Trap and G-Block Drill

This is an excellent drill for teaching the pulling guards to react to unforeseen blitzing and slanting by the defense.

The guards are lined up 8 yards from a defensive end holding a large stand-up dummy. Between the defensive end and guards are three other defenders holding hand dummies and located 1 yard off the line of scrimmage. As the guards pull and attempt to attack the defensive end, one of the three defenders holding hand dummies steps forward and knocks the pulling guard off stride. It is the offensive guard's responsibility to pick up this stunting defender. To add more flexibility to this drill, you may want to fake the step taken by the three defenders and let the guard kick out the end. By mixing up the two, this drill teaches your guards how to react in critical situations (see Figure 11.5).

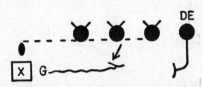

Figure 11.5   Guards Read Blitz.

Hand Blocking Drill

The offensive lineman is in a three-point stance. On the snap, he fires out into a dummy mounted on the one-man sled. Contact is made with the arms fully extended, butt low, and both legs positioned squarely underneath him. Once his body position has been checked, you give the command to push. At this time the blocker drives the dummy out 5 yards.

Once you are assured that all linemen have good blocking form, the pause that takes place after the first contact is eliminated, and the linemen hit and drive. You will find that this drill requires very good blocking form in order to move the sled. Form blocking in one area will limit the sled's movement.

BACKFIELD DRILLS

Shadow Drill

With his back turned the ball carrier is positioned 5 yards away from a defender. On the command "go" the defender starts at the ball carrier and tries to tackle him. On the second command given by you, the ball carrier turns around and tries to avoid being tackled. In order to protect the ball carrier, encourage him to pivot around and face the defender with a stiff arm before making any type of cut. Also, give the second command soon enough to avoid having the ball carrier being hit squarely (see Figure 11.6).

Figure 11.6   Ball Carriers Fake Out Defenders.

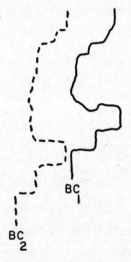

Figure 11.7   Second Ball Carrier Attempts to Catch First Ball Carrier.

Chase Drill

The chase drill emphasizes the "run to daylight" principle. One ball carrier lines up 2 yards back and 2 yards to one
side of another ball carrier. On the command "go" the first ball
carrier takes off in any forward direction he chooses and makes
as many cuts as he feels necessary to lose the trailing back. The
second back has to follow the first man's butt and stay with him.
This drill is done over a 40-yard area and conditions the athlete
as well as teaches him to follow his blocking (see Figure 11.7).

Set Down Drill

We use this drill for developing balance, a quick start, and
quick stop. The ball carrier sprints forward at full speed. On the
whistle, he lowers his center of gravity and comes to a complete
stop. On a hand signal given by you, the ball carrier sprints
laterally as fast as possible until another whistle blows. Again
the ball carrier lowers his center of gravity and comes to a stop.
This drill is repeated ten times over a distance of 40 yards (see
Figure 11.8).

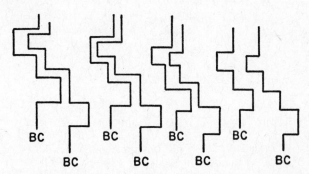

Figure 11.8   Ball Carriers Learn Balance and
Body Control.

Power Drill

The ball carrier lines up in front of the blaster. He takes the
handoff from the quarterback as he crashes through. As the ball
carrier comes out the other side, he runs between two defenders

holding air packs. One of the two defenders strikes out and attempts to knock the ball carrier over. The ball carrier does not know which defender will be hitting him so he must maintain body control as he explodes through (see Figure 11.9).

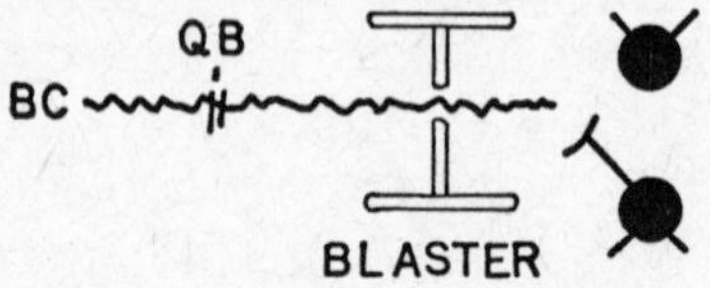

Figure 11.9   Ball Carrier Must Maintain Body Control.

Blast Drill

Two halfbacks line up side by side in a backfield position. On the snap, the lead back explodes through the blaster and blocks a defender holding an air pack. The trailing back takes the handoff from the quarterback, charges through the blaster, and reads the block made by the lead halfback (see Figure 11.10).

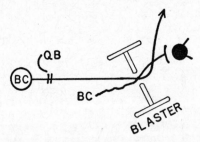

Figure 11.10   Ball Carrier Reads the First Back's Block.

High Step Drill

Using tires, the ball carrier starts with his right foot placed in the left tire. He crosses his left foot over into the right tire. Once this is done his right foot comes across his left foot and is placed on the ground to the outside. From this position, he places his left foot forward into the tire in front of him and crosses his right leg over his left foot (see Figure 11.11).

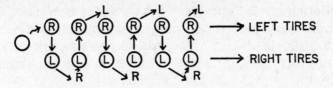

Figure 11.11   High Step Drill Develops Body Control.

This drill helps your backs develop tremendous balance and coordination. To add competition to this drill, you may wish to time each back to show improvement.

Hit, Spin, and React Drill

The ball carrier is positioned directly in front of two defenders holding stand-up dummies. They are 5 yards away and 5 yards apart. The back runs directly at the first dummy, hits and spins off, lifting his legs as high as possible. As contact is made on the first dummy, the second defender charges the ball carrier and tries to knock him off his feet. Once the ball carrier has spun off the first dummy and pivoted outside, he has to avoid the second dummy with a stiff arm (see Figure 11.12).

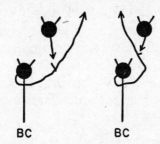

Figure 11.12   Hit, Spin, and Stiff Arm the Defender.

Control Drill

A defender grasps the ball carrier by the jersey at the top of the shoulder pads. Both players assume a slight crouch. As the ball carrier drives forward into the defender, the defender backs up as quickly as possible pulling first on one shoulder, then the other, attempting to pull the ball carrier to one side or to the ground. The control drill is conducted over a 40-yard distance. The only tool the ball carrier has is his free arm. The ball carrier may use this free arm to prevent himself from being pulled to the ground or maintain his balance (see Figure 11.13).

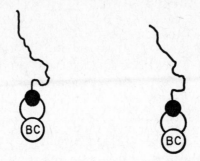

Figure 11.13   Defender Tries to Pull the Ball Carrier Off Balance.

Fake Drill

This drill is performed with two halfbacks in the split backfield position. Both backs dive into the guard holes to their side. At the snap, the quarterback hands off to one of the running backs and uses a reverse pivot to fake to the other. Two yards off the ball and in front of the quarterback is a defender holding an air pack. The defender attacks the back who he feels has the ball. The objective of this drill is to sharpen the faking ability of the ball carrier and quarterback (see Figure 11.14).

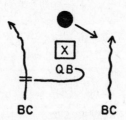

Figure 11.14   Ball Carriers and Quarterback Develop Faking Ability.

Quick Pitch and Dive Action Drill

This drill uses the quick pitch and dive action. When using this drill, the backs do not know who will get the ball. They will only be given the direction in which the play will be run. On the snap, the quarterback either quick pitches, dives the back, or throws a pass to the quick pitch receiver. This drill teaches both backs to carry out their fakes, execute the patterns properly, and block a defender if it becomes necessary (see Figure 11.15).

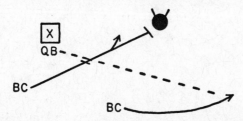

Figure 11.15   Developing the Quick Pitch Series.

Read and React Blocking Drill

The backs are lined up directly behind the guards. Outside the normal tackle holes defenders stand hand dummies. At the snap, both backs accelerate toward the middle defender. When the backs are within contact range, one of the three defenders fires out and attempts to knock the halfback over. This phase of the drill teaches the backs to react to various penetration within

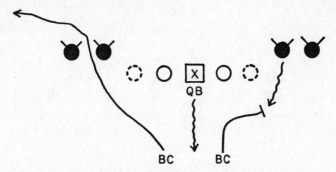

Figure 11.16   Developing Backfield Reads.

the interior line. If one of the defenders steps forward to make contact, the back runs through the line and executes a flare pattern. This is where the reading portion of the drill enters in (see Figure 11.16).

The read and react drill also uses the H-blocking scheme versus a boxing and crashing defensive end. In this drill the backs line up in a normal split backfield, and the defensive end is positioned in his normal location. At the snap, both backs head to the off-tackle hole. The lead back picks up the end (H-block) if he is crashing and the foreside back executes a flare pattern. If the end boxes, the foreside back will kick him out while the near (playside) back executes a flare pattern [see Figure 11.17 (a) and (b)].

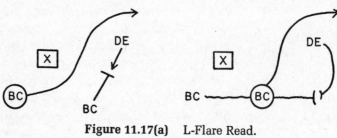

Figure 11.17(a)   L-Flare Read.

Figure 11.17(b)   R-Flare Read.

Leapfrog Drill

The leapfrog drill uses all running backs, each positioned one behind the other. All members of this drill carry a football (tucked under arm) and are positioned in a three-point stance. The last man at the end of the line runs forward, places his free arm on the man in front, and leaps over each member in line. When he has leaped over every player, he assumes the lead. This drill is performed over a 200-yard area. Each member is spaced 5 yards apart. The only tool that the ball carrier can use to keep his balance is his free arm (see Figure 11.18).

Figure 11.18   Leapfrog Drill.

QUARTERBACK AND RECEIVER DRILLS

The timing between the quarterback and receivers is very important. When performing these drills, both groups always work together.

Hot Drill

The hot drill uses three receivers and two halfbacks. Each member of this five-man group wears a different colored scrimmage vest over a white practice jersey. In the huddle, the quarterback gives only the formation. At the line of scrimmage, he calls five single-digit numbers. At the snap, the quarterback drops back into his normal position. Once he has set his back foot, you call out a color. The quarterback then has to readjust his feet in order to throw the ball to the specific receiver. After the first pass has been thrown, you immediately give him another ball. The quarterback has to reposition his feet again and throw to the deepest receiver that was called by the quarterback at the line of scrimmage. This drill teaches the quarterback to react quickly and to know where every receiver is during a pattern (see Figure 11.19).

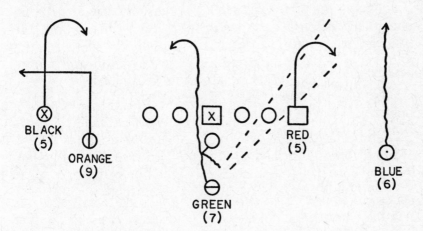

Figure 11.19   Red—First Ball . . . Green—
Second Ball.

Locate the Receiver Drill

Stretch a piece of canvas 20 feet long and 7 feet high. At a 45 degree angle, position two pieces 10 feet long and 7 feet high. This obstruction should be placed so that the quarterback cannot see the receivers. This drill works toward developing two areas:

1. Since the quarterback cannot see his receivers, he must develop a mental picture of where each receiver is located once the cuts are made.
2. The receivers do not see the ball being thrown until it has crossed over the canvas.

This teaches the receivers to react to a poorly thrown ball. When using this drill, all receivers are positioned in front of the obstacle. The quarterback is behind the obstacle and makes his calls from this position. This drill is extremely effective for developing timing between the quarterbacks and receivers. It is particularly effective in developing receivers who have a hard time picking up the thrown pass (see Figure 11.20).

Read the Open Zone Drill

Facing the offense is a mock defense holding hand dummies. This defense includes only defensive backs and linebackers. In the huddle, the quarterback calls only the formation followed by a read call. After breaking the huddle and coming up to the line, the quarterback calls out the defense being used. On the snap, the quarterback drops back and watches the zones open up. When he is in the set position, he throws into an open zone. It is the responsibility of the receiver in that zone to locate the pass and catch it. By continuously using this drill, your quarterback and receivers develop a second sense in determining where cuts should be made in order to take advantage of a specific defense. You will find that this drill sharpens your passing game to the point where your quarterback is completing passes in the tightest situation (see Figure 11.21).

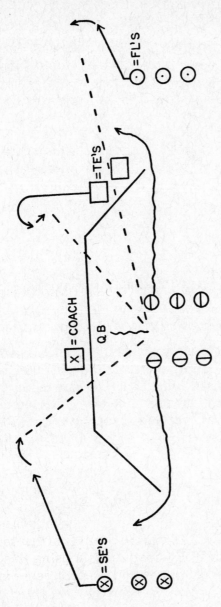

Figure 11.20 Locating a Blind Receiver.

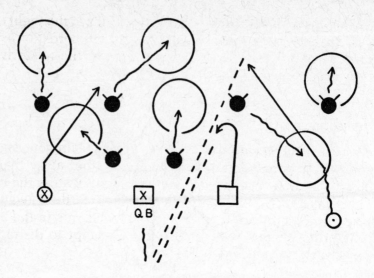

Figure 11.21   Reading the Defense as it Opens Up.

Bandit Drill

Two receivers are lined up side by side 1 yard apart. Both receivers run the same pattern. On the snap, both receivers start downfield and make their cut at a 10-yard marker. The quarterback tries to place the ball in between the two receivers. The object is to see which receiver comes up with the ball. This drill

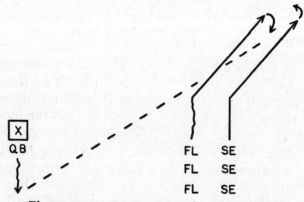

Figure 11.22   Receivers Develop Their Catching Skills.

teaches the receivers to come forward or back to the flight of the pass. It also teaches them to run their patterns correctly, as they should end up fairly close to each other when the ball arrives in between them (see Figure 11.22).

Interference Drill

The receivers are split into two groups facing one another at about 15 yards. One line is 2 yards further away than the other. The first receiver in each line runs towards the other. The ball is thrown to the receiver who is the farthest away. The player in the closest line jumps, puts his hands in the air, or yells at the player behind him in an attempt to distract his concentration (see Figure 11.23).

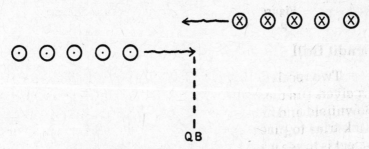

Figure 11.23   First Receiver Tries to Distract Second Receiver.

Fly Drill

The receivers are divided into two groups. One group lines up on the 40-yard line one behind the other on the right side-line. The other group is at the goal line on the opposite side of the field lined up one behind the other. On the quarterback's command from each group, the receivers run down the sideline as fast as possible. The quarterback takes a five-step drop, plants, and throws as high and as far as possible. The receivers run to the ball and wait for it to come to them. Once a receiver has caught the ball, he sprints to the other group on the opposite side (see Figure 11.24).

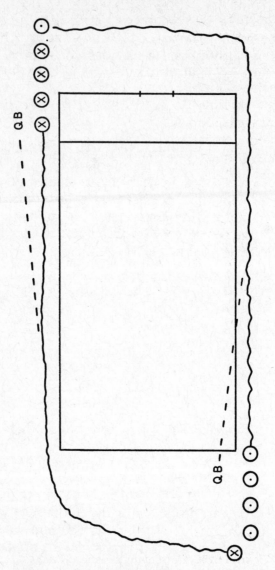

Figure 11.24 Teaches Receivers to Run Under the Pass Rather Than Reach.

Progression Drill

There are three groups, consisting of three receivers and two halfbacks. Against this offensive unit is a mock defense consisting of linebackers and defensive backs. The first group has called a play, executed it, and started back behind group three. The second group has watched the first group execute their play. The quarterback in the second group has to select a play that specifically attacks a vulnerable area left vacant by the defense on the previous play. Once group two has successfully executed its play, group three follows. This progression continues until the defense has successfully stopped the offense two consecutive times (see Figure 11.25).

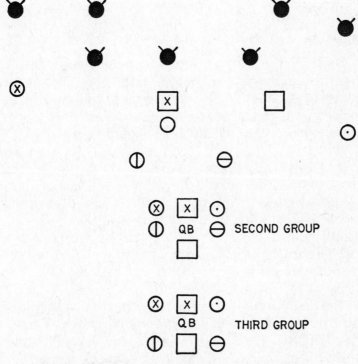

Figure 11.25   Developing a Planned Progression of Plays.

Perfect Plays—Two-Minute Drill

The two-minute drill enables our offense to work under pressure. It forces the athletes to hustle in and out of the huddle and execute their patterns exactly to specifications. When using this drill, we break our offense into three groups. Each group maintains ball control until four downs are used without a first down or the two minutes run out. This is a competition drill between the three groups to see which group can move the ball most effectively. In the huddle, the quarterback calls two plays. One of these plays should be called to pick up 10 yards or get the ball out of bounds. At this time, the chains move and the offense can huddle, or time is called by the coach running the clock. This particular drill is an excellent conditioner. We generally run this drill after a heavy practice. The offense has to give it everything they have when they are tired.

Communication Drill

Under game situations you may have a special play in mind. If your team has not practiced the play, your chances of successfully executing it are minimal. We use a drill that teaches our quarterbacks to read a play given on a 3 by 5 card, explain it to the team in the huddle, and execute it.

When using this drill, each quarterback calls a timeout. He comes to the sideline, picks up the card, looks at it, and returns to the huddle. If any questions exist after the quarterback looks at the play, he asks them and returns to the huddle as quickly as possible. By looking at the card and returning to the huddle, the quarterback has ample time to discuss it with the rest of the team. The drill has given our coaching staff a tremendous amount of success in calling plays that have resulted in touchdowns.

The drills presented are drills that develop specific phases of this offense plus teach each individual athlete how to read certain situations. Although there are many other drills used to develop the individual athletes, we, as a coaching staff, feel that these drills benefit this offense as a whole.

INDEX

THE PRO-T OFFENSE

WINNING FOOTBALL WITH A MODERN PASSING ATTACK

MIKE McDANIELS

"The Pro-T Offense…has something for everyone. The beginning coach could use it as his playbook and the experienced coach can use it for ideas. Mike McDaniels has done an excellent job in organizing his offensive approach to football."

Don James
Head Football Coach
University of Washington

This guide presents one of the most explosive offenses ever conceived—the Pro-T—now adapted especially for high school play. It uses a combination of two wide receivers and a tight end to make your team both a short-range and long-range passing threat. What's more, the Pro-T incorporates a progression of running plays designed to add balance and flexibility to your total offensive arsenal.

HOW THE PRO-T OFFENSE WORKS

The Pro-T Offense relies on multiple formations and a series of basic plays like the dive, sweep, off-tackle, quick pitch and trap. It gives you:

• the ability to spread the defense by forcing it to give up specific areas of the field…

• a progression attack that lets you take advantage of the open zone with a short post pattern to the flanker…

• patterns that let your offense flood the field while still maintaining excellent quarterback coverage…

and much more.